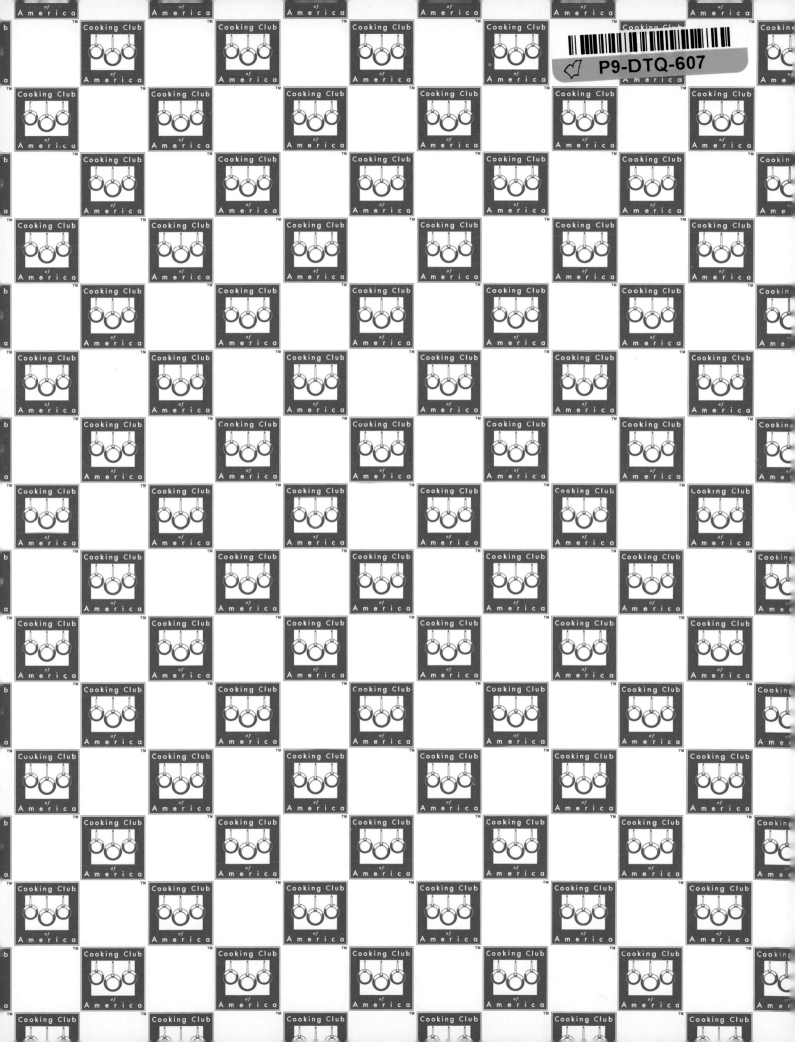

COOKING ESSENTIALS

COOKING ARTS COLLECTION™

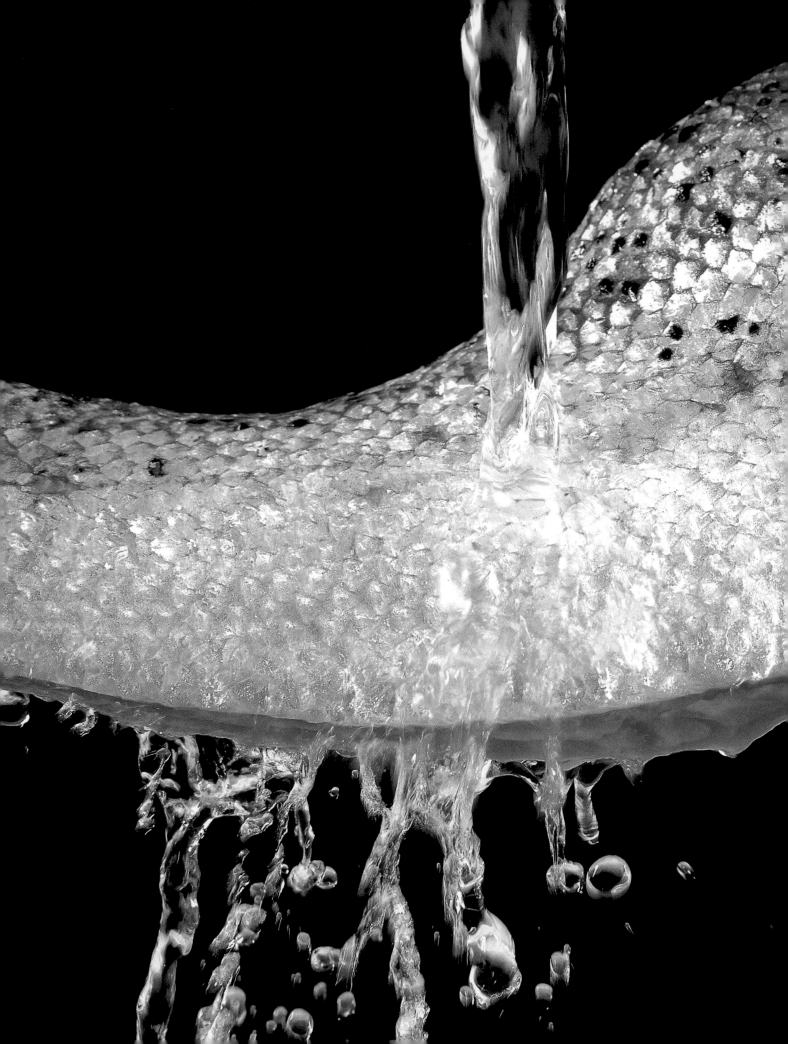

COOKING ESSENTIALS

MARY BERRY
MARLENA SPIELER

PHOTOGRAPHY BY DAVE KING

SPECIAL EDITION FOR THE
COOKING CLUB OF AMERICA™

COOKING ESSENTIALS

COOKING ARTS COLLECTION™

Mike Vail
**Vice President, Product Marketing and
Business Development**

Tom Carpenter
**Director of Book and
New Media Development**

Heather Koshiol
Book Development Coordinator

30 29 28 27 26 25

First American Edition, 1997

Published in the United States by
DK Publishing, Inc.
375 Hudson Street
New York, New York 10014
www.dk.com

ISBN 978-0-7894-7067-6

Reproduced in Italy by GRB
Printed and bound in China

CONTENTS

PANTRY 10

*Advice on how to create a stock of useful ingredients
that you can draw on from day to day.*

EQUIPMENT 20

*A practical guide to avoiding expensive mistakes
when equipping your kitchen.*

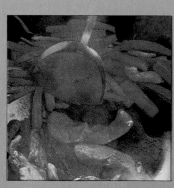

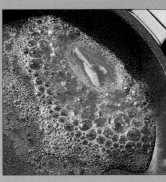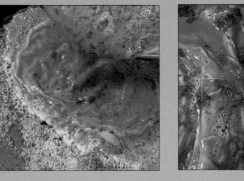

TECHNIQUES 32

These techniques are the building blocks the beginner will use to construct the recipes that follow. Mastering these simple basic skills will ensure culinary success now and for many years to come.

MASTER RECIPES 72

Each of these Master Recipes is fully explained in step-by-step pictures, with information on special equipment and ingredients, and cook's tips from the experts.

RECIPE REPERTOIRE 118

A resource of essential recipes for the new cook, drawing on the skills learned in the Techniques and Master Recipes sections to create an impressive culinary range.

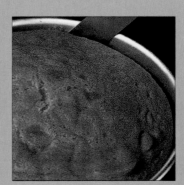

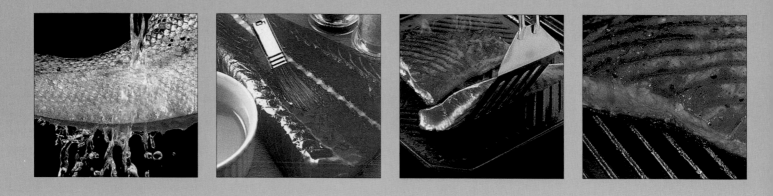

INTRODUCTION

BEING A GOOD COOK doesn't just happen. It starts with knowledge. And that knowledge must run deeper than just a recipe on a page, no matter how much or little cooking experience you have.

Successful cooking starts with knowing the ingredients you work with and understanding the tools and equipment you use. Good cooking techniques bring those two factors together, and recipes offer the ideas you need to blend it all into great food.

Simply enough, that's the story behind *Cooking Essentials*. Cooking should be as easy and uncomplicated as possible. We want you to have fun with your cooking, be successful and really enjoy the results.

So this book is for you if you've been cooking for a long time, for it will bring you new cooking knowledge and ideas. And this book is for you if you're just starting out cooking, or are ready to take that next step into really knowing this most delightful of endeavors.

Here's how *Cooking Essentials* does it, keeping an eye for the fresher, lighter food of today.

We start with a visual guide to the pantry, describing and explaining a key choice of ingredients from peppercorns, oils, and vinegars, to pasta and beans, vanilla beans and honey. A stock of good, basic ingredients will help you cook well, and for those on a budget, this section will ensure

that bad buys are kept to a minimum and that correct storage will prevent waste.

Next, we offer advice on saving money as you set up or improve your kitchen. To help you avoid expensive mistakes, we devote a section to kitchen tools and equipment. It will allow you to identify which items are most practical and versatile and which items are worth investing in for the long term. Why buy a cheap set of bad knives when just two or three good ones will do and will last forever? What are the most useful small appliances to buy? Good-quality machines are expensive, so you need to choose wisely.

A portfolio of essential Techniques forms a vital reference source. You'll be surprised at all the tricks and techniques you can use to make your cooking more efficient and enjoyable. You will turn to this section again and again.

The Master Recipes are designed to be your keys to even better cooking, allowing you to utilize a wide range of essential cooking skills. You'll find secrets to making an omelet truly fluffy and a creamy soup wonderfully smooth, roasting a chicken to perfection, baking the perfect apple pie and more. All the recipes are easy to follow and will help you cook with confidence for any occasion.

Last but not least, there is the Recipe Repertoire, a collection of our favorite recipes that we hope will become yours too. Here you will find some time-honored classics with a modern twist, and some new and imaginative ideas using the latest ingredients available in our supermarkets.

Enjoy *Cooking Essentials*, your companion on the never-ending road to more cooking knowledge and better cooking.

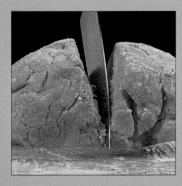

HOW TO USE THIS BOOK

The sections of this book are designed to be used in conjunction

with one another. Always read through all the relevant information

before you begin. All recipes serve four unless otherwise stated.

■ MASTER RECIPES

These twelve Master Recipes use the basic techniques
shown in the Techniques section and teach the new cook
the key skills he or she will need to build up a whole culinary
repertoire. We recommend that you start with these recipes.

*Each Master Recipe has a close-up
shot to inspire you and to show you
exactly what you should expect to see
as your dish progresses.*

*The Keys to Success
contain vital information.
Read them carefully
before you begin.*

*Cook's Notes contains tips
on preparation, serving,
and nutritional values.*

*Cross-references to all the
techniques you will need
appear in the bottom-left-
hand corner of the page.*

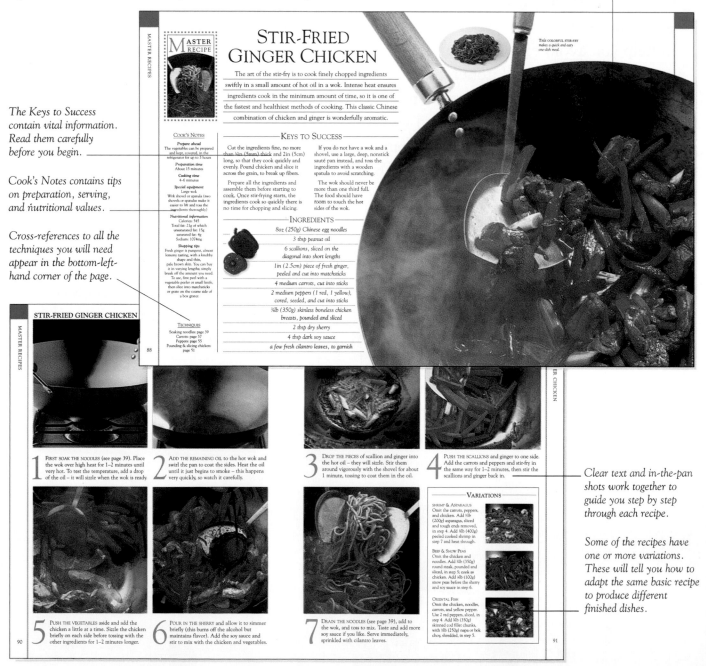

*Clear text and in-the-pan
shots work together to
guide you step by step
through each recipe.*

*Some of the recipes have
one or more variations.
These will tell you how to
adapt the same basic recipe
to produce different
finished dishes.*

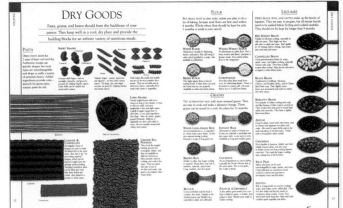

▪ EQUIPMENT

All the recipes in this book use the equipment illustrated in this section, so to achieve the best results you should try to use the same kind of equipment.

▪ PANTRY

This section tells you about useful ingredients to keep in your pantry or kitchen cabinets. You won't need them all, so buy as you need them and you will gradually build up a useful stock.

▪ TECHNIQUES

This part of the book will teach you all the basic techniques needed to create the recipes that come later. Although the Master Recipes contain cross-references to the Techniques, the Recipe Repertoire does not. If you come across an unfamiliar technique in the Repertoire, look it up in the index; you will be referred either to this section or to the Master Recipes.

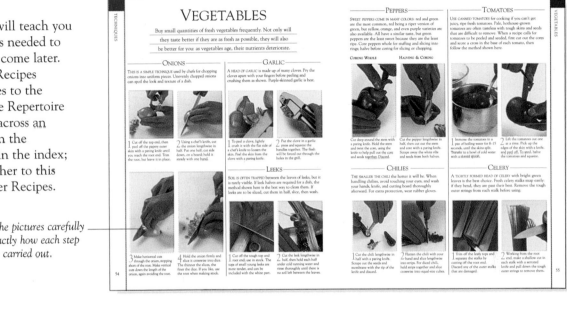

Look at the pictures carefully to see exactly how each step should be carried out.

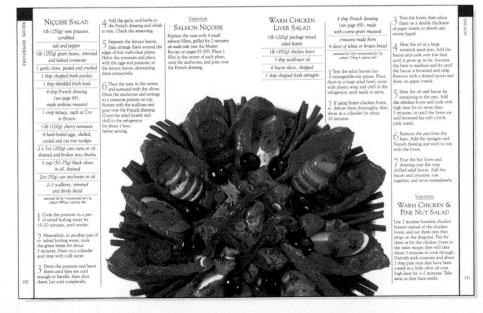

▪ RECIPE REPERTOIRE

The Recipe Repertoire contains recipes that show you how to use your newly acquired skills to create a host of classic and imaginative dishes.

─ IMPORTANT NOTES ─

▪ Measurements and weights are given in this book in imperial and metric units. Imperial and metric units are not interchangeable; use one or the other throughout the recipe. Never mix them.

▪ Sometimes the recipes call for butter, margarine, or oil for greasing. This is not specified in the ingredients list, so always check that you have enough before you begin.

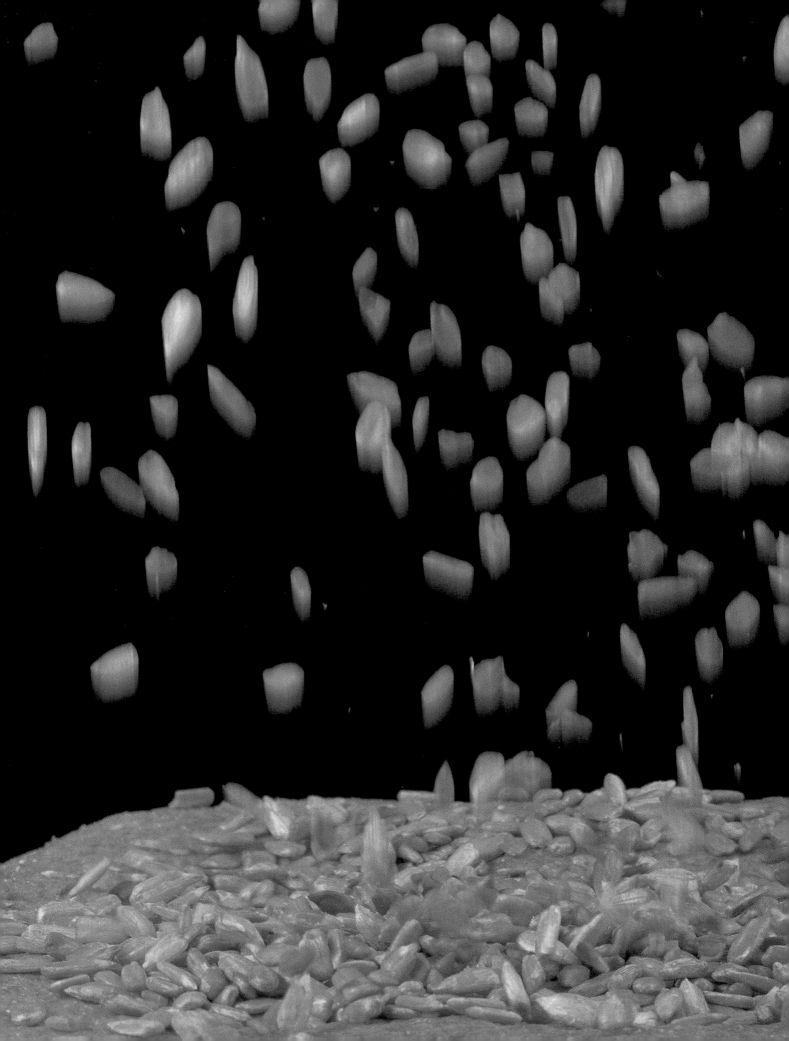

BEFORE STOCKING UP, think about the meals you are most likely to cook, then buy only those things that you know you are going to use. For storing food, use a cabinet that is in the coolest part of your kitchen – against a north-facing wall is best, but certainly not next to the oven, radiator, or boiler. Make sure the cabinet is dry, and line the shelves with wipe-clean material. Pack the shelves logically – bags of flour together, alongside packages of rice and pasta, for example – with the things that you use most often within easy reach at the front. Regularly check the expiration dates on packages, bottles, and cans, and also check for foods that have to be refrigerated once opened.

PANTRY

DRY GOODS

Pasta, grains, and beans should form the backbone of your pantry. They keep well in a cool, dry place and provide the building blocks for an infinite variety of nutritious meals.

PASTA

DRIED PASTA KEEPS for 2 years if kept cool and dry. Authentic recipes use specific shapes, but most types are interchangeable and shape is really a matter of personal choice. Added ingredients provide color – spinach for green pasta, tomato paste for red.

SHORT SHAPES

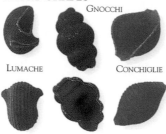

GNOCCHI

LUMACHE

CONCHIGLIE

Concave shell shapes, such as conchiglie, lumache, and gnocchi, are good for holding chunky sauces. Giant shells can be stuffed and served with a sauce.

MACARONI

PENNE

Tubular shapes – penne, macaroni, and rigatoni – are best with creamy sauces. The large, fat, and ridged varieties are good for trapping chunky and meaty sauces.

FARFALLE

FUSILLI

Solid shapes like fusilli and farfalle are two of the most popular short pastas. They are versatile and go with most sauces, especially those made with cream or vegetables.

SPAGHETTI

LONG SHAPES

Sturdy spaghetti goes with most sauces as long as any chunks of meat or fish are small; narrower spaghettini is best with light sauces. Capelli d'angelo (angel hair) is ultra-fine, so toss with ingredients that cling – olive oil, butter, pepper, grated Parmesan. Ribbons of tagliatelle are often sold coiled in nests; they are usually served with robust meat sauces.

NEST OF TAGLIATELLE

LASAGNE & CANNELLONI

Rectangular sheets of lasagne are used to make the baked dish of the same name. Best buy is the "no precooking required" lasagne, which can be layered straight from the package without boiling. Packaged cannelloni tubes can be filled after they have been boiled and cooled, then baked in a tomato or white sauce.

LASAGNE

CANNELLONI

CHINESE EGG NOODLES

These look like tangled knitting pressed into rectangular shapes, and they are available in different thicknesses. Most varieties need no cooking; just soak in hot water. They are quick and easy to use in stir-fries and soups, and good to accompany other Asian dishes.

FLOUR

BUY SMALL BAGS to start with, unless you plan to do a lot of baking, because most flours are best used within 6 months. Whole-wheat flour should be kept for only 2 months; it tends to turn rancid.

WHITE FLOUR
All-purpose is useful for thickening, batters, and pastry. Buy self-rising for cakes only if specified in a recipe. Also available as unbleached.

WHOLE-WHEAT FLOUR
An alternative to white flour. Has a nutty texture and flavor, and gives a heavier result. Store whole-wheat flour in the refrigerator.

BREAD FLOUR
This higher gluten flour is best for making bread: if other flours are used the bread may not rise properly. Available as white and whole-wheat.

CORNSTARCH
Very fine white flour made from corn, for thickening liquids. Needs to be mixed to a paste with cold water before use or it will form lumps.

GRAINS

TRY ALTERNATING RICE with more unusual grains. They are easy to cook and make a pleasant change. These grains can be stored in a cool, dry place for 12 months.

WHITE LONG-GRAIN RICE
An accompaniment to, or ingredient in, many main-course dishes. Grains stay separate during cooking. Basmati is a type of long-grain rice.

INSTANT RICE
Alternative to white or brown rice. Grains are polished or parboiled and they never stick, so are easy to cook. Available as long and medium grain.

BROWN RICE
Similar to white, but longer cooking is required. Nutty flavor and rich in vitamins, minerals, and protein. Long, medium, and short grain.

COUSCOUS
An accompaniment to savory dishes, especially the North African dish of the same name. Not a true grain, but a type of pasta.

BULGUR
Comes preboiled until the husk is cracked, then dried. Popular in the Mediterranean and Middle East, especially in pilafs and tabbouleh.

POLENTA (CORNMEAL)
A fine yellow grain made from corn that is boiled in water, or boiled, then grilled or fried. Widely used staple in Italian cooking.

LEGUMES

DRIED BEANS, PEAS, AND LENTILS make up the family of legumes. They are easy to prepare, but all except lentils need to be soaked before boiling and cooked carefully. They should not be kept for longer than 9 months.

RED KIDNEY BEANS
Popular in Mexican cooking, especially in chili con carne. Their bright red skins add color to salads and stews. Boil rapidly for 10 minutes before cooking, then drain and cook with fresh water.

CANNELLINI BEANS
Good general-purpose beans for soups, salads, stews, and Italian cooking, especially Tuscan-style soups. They have a fluffy texture when cooked. May also be referred to as fagioli or white kidney beans.

BLACK BEANS
Traditional in Caribbean, Mexican, Chinese, and Brazilian dishes, and in Cuban black bean soup. Their slightly sweet flavor goes particularly well with rice dishes and spicy sauces.

BORLOTTI BEANS
Very popular in Italian cooking and soups and dips because of their creamy consistency. Their streaky skins look good in mixed bean salads and casseroles. They have a slightly bittersweet flavor.

ADZUKI
Good in salads, mixed with other beans, and in Chinese and Japanese rice dishes and soups. Also used in sweet dishes and as the main ingredient of red bean paste. Tender with a strong flavor when cooked.

CHICKPEAS
Most familiar in hummus, falafel, and other Middle Eastern dishes, but also used in Indian curries and long-cooking Spanish casseroles. They need the longest soaking and cooking time of all the beans.

SPLIT PEAS
Yellow and green can be used interchangeably in soups, purées, and stews. Green split peas are sometimes served cooked to a purée and seasoned to accompany roasts and fish dishes.

LENTILS
Red or orange lentils are used for making soups, and Indian curries called dhal. They lose their shape and become mushy in consistency when cooked. Green, Puy, and brown lentils keep their shape and make excellent quick vegetable side dishes.

SPICES, SEASONINGS & HERBS

Freshly ground spices are intense in flavor but quickly lose

their pungency, so buy them as you need them in small quantities and

store any leftover powder in airtight containers in a dark place.

SPICES & SEEDS

SPICE SEEDS SHOULD be left whole until you are ready to use them. Dry-cooking for 2–3 minutes will heighten their flavor: put seeds in a wok or sauté pan and toss vigorously over high heat. You do not need to add any oil. Other seeds, particularly sesame, can also be dry-cooked to enhance their flavor.

CORIANDER
FLAVOR *Highly aromatic, with a mild hint of orange peel.*
USE *Whole seeds, or ground, in Indian dishes, with poultry, meat, and vegetables, especially carrots.*

TURMERIC
FLAVOR *Musky, peppery.*
USE *Mainly sold ground. Use to color foods yellow, especially Indian curries and bean dishes. Use sparingly as an alternative to saffron.*

CLOVES
FLAVOR *Sweet, highly aromatic.*
USE *Stud onions, oranges, and baked hams with whole cloves to decorate and flavor; use ground in desserts and baking, and with fruit.*

CARDAMOM
FLAVOR *Strong, with a lingering lemonlike aftertaste.*
USE *In Indian and Middle Eastern cooking, especially sweet dishes. Split pods and remove seeds to use.*

CUMIN
FLAVOR *Very distinctive, slightly bitter, a little like caraway.*
USE *In Mexican, African, and Indian food, and with chicken and vegetables. Difficult to crush at home.*

CINNAMON
FLAVOR *Subtle, spicy-sweet.*
USE *Ground when poaching fruit, and in pies, cakes, and cookies. Infuse sticks in sugar syrups, milk and custards, and mulled wines.*

GINGER
FLAVOR *Hot, pungent, warming.*
USE *In desserts and baking, pickles and chutneys, and in Indian and Chinese spice mixtures. Can be used as a substitute for fresh ginger.*

SAFFRON
FLAVOR *Pungent, aromatic, sometimes faintly bitter.*
USE *Traditionally a very highly sought-after spice, made from the dried stigmas of certain crocus flowers. Used for coloring foods yellow, especially rice and fish dishes, sweet breads, and cookies. Soak threads in warm water for 20 minutes, strain, and use liquid. Alternatively, sprinkle powder directly into liquids and stir to avoid streaking.*

NUTMEG
FLAVOR *Sweet, warm, quite powerful. More pungent if grated fresh whenever it is needed, preferably at the end of cooking.*
USE *In sweet dishes, in savory sauces, and with vegetables. Mace, more expensive and more refined in flavor than nutmeg, is the lacy outer covering. Use to infuse sauces and soups, shellfish, and cheese dishes. Like the nutmeg itself, this is available either whole – pressed flat and dried – or ground.*

MACE

CARAWAY SEEDS
FLAVOR *Pungent, bittersweet.*
USE *In Austrian and German soups, stews, vegetable dishes; in breads, especially rye, and baked goods. Good with cheese and sausages.*

WHITE SESAME SEEDS
FLAVOR *Mildly nutty, best recognized in tahini paste made from ground white sesame seeds.*
USE *In Middle Eastern and Chinese cooking. Often used toasted.*

POPPY SEEDS
FLAVOR *Nutty, slightly sweet.*
USE *In baking and Indian dishes, as a garnish for salads, noodles, and vegetables. Gray-blue seeds are most common. Can be used toasted.*

DILL SEEDS
FLAVOR *Lingering, with a hint of aniseed similar to caraway.*
USE *In Scandinavian and Eastern European cooking with fish, pickled cucumber, vegetables. Also in breads.*

THE PEPPER FAMILY

MANY PEPPERS are made from dried capsicums. These are different from everyday pepper, which is ground from peppercorns. Different pepper products vary in heat, so it is wise to know which is which.

DRIED HOT PEPPERS

PAPRIKA
FLAVOR *The mildest of the pepper family. Available in sweet (mild) and hot forms. Sweet is most useful.*
USE *In Hungarian and Spanish dishes, and as a colorful garnish.*

CAYENNE
FLAVOR *Made from one of the hottest varieties of chilies.*
USE *In Mexican and Cajun dishes, and to add piquancy and heat to other foods according to taste.*

HOT PEPPER FLAKES
FLAVOR *Very fiery with lots of seeds, so use with caution.*
USE *Sprinkle sparingly in or over foods, before or after cooking. Make it yourself at home by crushing dried hot red peppers in a mortar.*

CHILI POWDER
FLAVOR *In fact a blend of chilies, garlic, cumin, and oregano. Different brands will vary in heat.*
USE *For authentic Mexican, Indian, and Southwestern dishes.*

SPICE MIXTURES

READY-MADE blends of ground spices are time-saving, economical, and very handy to have in the pantry. The choice is vast, and mixtures vary according to individual manufacturers and brands. The three shown here are the most commonly used.

CURRY POWDER
FLAVOR *Varies from Indian through Chinese to Thai, some perfumed and mild, others hot.*
USE *Gives curries an authentic flavor, which is often difficult to achieve by mixing spices yourself.*

GARAM MASALA
FLAVOR *Usually a mix of cumin, coriander, cardamom, cloves, cinnamon, pepper, mace, and bay.*
USE *In curries, particularly north Indian, which are mild and perfumed rather than fiery and hot.*

PIE SPICE
FLAVOR *Traditional mixture of ground sweet spices, usually allspice, cinnamon, cloves, coriander, mace, and nutmeg.*
USE *Mainly as a seasoning for pies, cookies, and cakes.*

15

SALT & PEPPER

THESE ARE ESSENTIAL in the kitchen, both for cooking and as table condiments. There are many different types – these are the most useful.

TABLE SALT
TYPE *Refined salt with anti-caking agents. Free-flowing.*
USE *For cooking and at the table. Better than the less refined kitchen or cooking salt, which tends to clog and is not fine enough for table use.*

COARSE SALT
TYPE *Large or medium-size crystals. Choose kosher or sea salt; sea salt tastes slightly stronger.*
USE *For cooking and at the table. A salt mill is often used to grind large crystals, but this is not essential.*

BLACK PEPPER
TYPE *Whole peppercorns and ground black pepper.*
USE *For freshness, grind peppercorns in a pepper mill when you need them. Pre-ground is useful for seasoning large quantities of food.*

MIXED PEPPERCORNS
TYPE *A blend of whole black, white, pink, green peppercorns. Five-pepper blends include allspice berries.*
USE *For grinding in or over food. A spicy and attractive alternative to black or white peppercorns.*

DRIED HERBS

FRESH HERBS are preferable to dried in salads and sauces, but dried herbs are often better in dishes like casseroles and stews that require long cooking, so a small stock of dried herbs is essential.
Freeze-dried herbs have a good aroma, color, and flavor, but their flavor is generally concentrated, so use half the quantity of dried to fresh. To store, keep them in airtight containers in the dark, or at least away from sunlight. Aroma and flavor should stay fresh for up to 12 months.

SAGE
FLAVOR *Slightly bitter, stronger than fresh sage.*
USE *Good with meat, especially fatty pork, duck, and sausages, and with veal and variety meats. Also good in egg and cheese dishes. Use sparingly.*

DILL
FLAVOR *Subtle, tones of aniseed. Less pungent than fresh.*
USE *For marinades and dressings, especially in Northern and Eastern European cooking with cucumber, fish, and root vegetables.*

OREGANO
FLAVOR *Powerful, almost spicy. A variety of wild marjoram.*
USE *In Mediterranean and Italian dishes – with tomatoes, in pasta sauces, and on pizza. Also frequently used in Mexican cooking.*

BAY
FLAVOR *Pungent, resinous; stronger if leaves are torn before use. Long cooking releases flavor best.*
USE *In stocks, sauces, soups, and stews. For infusing milk and in bouquets garni. Also good with fish.*

MIXED HERBS
FLAVOR *Usually a mixture of marjoram, oregano, rosemary, summer savory, and thyme.*
USE *In sauces and stews, cooked tomato dishes, sprinkled over pizza. Can be used in most savory dishes.*

BASIL
FLAVOR *Sweet, spicy. Slightly more minty than fresh basil.*
USE *In salads and long-cooking Mediterranean sauces and casseroles, especially with tomatoes. Traditionally partnered with garlic.*

ROSEMARY
FLAVOR *Pungent, spicy yet refreshing. Milder than fresh rosemary.*
USE *In casseroles and marinades with lamb, pork, chicken, and with potatoes. Used in Italian dishes and to flavor bread, such as focaccia.*

OILS & VINEGARS

Rows of different bottles of glistening oils and vinegars make a

spectacular display, but only a few of the more versatile types are

really necessary to bring out the best in your cooking.

OILS

USED FOR FRYING, brushing, basting, marinades, and dressings, oils are made from vegetables, fruit, nuts, or seeds and are healthier than animal fats. Store in a cool place and check labels for storage times – they vary.

VINEGARS

BOTTLED VINEGARS ARE A GOOD BUY, but don't display them on the kitchen windowsill or they will quickly lose their flavor. Store somewhere cool and dark, and they will taste good for up to 2 years.

SUNFLOWER OIL
FLAVOR *Very light and neutral, virtually tasteless.*
USE *General-purpose oil that can be used for all cooking purposes. Good mixed half and half with olive oil for extra flavor.*

OLIVE OIL
FLAVOR *Mildly fruity, but brands vary. "Virgin" is good; it has a low acidity level and is less refined.*
USE *In Mediterranean dishes, marinades, broiling, barbecuing, and sautéing.*

EXTRA-VIRGIN OLIVE OIL
FLAVOR *Peppery, fruity. From the first cold pressing.*
USE *For dressing salads and cold dishes, and sprinkling over hot foods just before serving.*

WINE VINEGAR
FLAVOR *Red and white are mildly fruity; sherry is nutty and brown. Balsamic is oak-matured and musky.*
USE *In dressings, sauces, and marinades. Use less of balsamic – it is strong.*

CIDER VINEGAR
FLAVOR *Strong, like an acidic hard cider.*
USE *As wine vinegar, but has a stronger taste, so use less. Use with pork, liver, sausages, and in pickles, chutneys, and dressings.*

17

CONDIMENTS & PRESERVED FOOD

For use at the table and as quick-and-easy instant flavorings, bottled sauces and preserves are well worth using. Check labels for storage directions – some need to be kept in the refrigerator once opened.

SAUCES & PRESERVES

ADD A DASH of soy sauce, a drop of Tabasco, or a spoonful of ketchup, and the flavor of a dish can be transformed. There is a huge variety of sauces and preserves on the market, and it is a matter of personal taste which you choose to keep in stock.

TABASCO SAUCE
FLAVOR *Fiery hot, made from a secret recipe based on hot peppers.*
USE *In Mexican cooking, and to give a kick to any bland food.*

HORSERADISH SAUCE
FLAVOR *Pungent, hot horseradish root with vinegar and cream.*
USE *With beef, cold meats, smoked fish, chicken, and eggs.*

WORCESTERSHIRE SAUCE
FLAVOR *Piquant, salty, with anchovies, molasses, tamarind.*
USE *To spice up bland foods, sauces, marinades, and dressings.*

TOMATO KETCHUP
FLAVOR *Unique blend of tomatoes, vinegar, and sugar.*
USE *In marinades, dressings, stews, sauces, and relishes.*

SOY SAUCE
FLAVOR *Chinese light soy is mild; dark is strong and salty. Japanese soy is less salty and slightly sweet.*
USE *In Asian dishes and stir-fries.*

MANGO CHUTNEY
FLAVOR *Fruity, sweet, with chunks of mango. Some are hot and spicy.*
USE *In Indian dishes, dressings, sauces. With cheese and mayonnaise.*

REDCURRANT JELLY
FLAVOR *Very sweet.*
USE *To add sweetness and color to gravies and sauces, especially with pork, poultry, and game.*

MUSTARD

MADE FROM THE SEEDS of the mustard plant, mustard appears in many different flavors, colors, and textures. Everyone has his own favorites, and any of them can be used in cooking or as a condiment. The three shown here provide a good contrast in flavors and textures.

DIJON
FLAVOR *Strong, made from the hottest mustard seeds.*
USE *In sauces, dips, dressings, mayonnaise, and marinades.*

COARSE-GRAIN
FLAVOR *Usually mild, but some types are hot. Sometimes vinegary.*
USE *As for Dijon, for a milder flavor and crunchier texture.*

DRY
FLAVOR *Very hot, pungent.*
USE *Add powder to sauces, dips, marinades. Or mix to a paste with cold water and use as for Dijon.*

TOMATOES

FRESH TOMATOES are always available, but often lack flavor. Whole or chopped canned tomatoes in natural juice taste good all year round and make a good substitute. These tomato-based products are also useful for adding richness and depth.

SUN-DRIED TOMATOES IN OIL
TYPE *Halves or pieces, packed in olive oil in jars or sold loose.*
USE *In salads, sauces, and stews.*

CONCENTRATES
TYPE *Purée and paste. Sun-dried paste has a mellow, sweet flavor.*
USE *For flavoring, coloring, and thickening sauces, soups, and stews.*

CRUSHED TOMATOES
TYPE *Strained crushed tomatoes in cans, bottles, and waxed boxes.*
USE *In sauces, soups, and stews; for a smooth, thick consistency.*

DESSERTS & BAKING ESSENTIALS

SWEETENERS

WHITE SUGAR
Superfine is good for cooking – it is fine and dissolves quickly; granulated is coarser, and best for table use.

BROWN SUGAR
Light and dark; both are refined, with molasses added. Use instead of white sugar for color and flavor, especially in baked goods.

CONFECTIONERS' SUGAR
Powdered refined sugar for icings and sweet sauces. Also for sifting over desserts, pies, and cakes for decorative effect.

RAW SUGAR
Crunchy brown sugar. Crystals do not dissolve easily, but give a good texture if sprinkled over cakes and cookies before baking.

MAPLE SYRUP
Use in ice cream, cakes, and cookies, also to pour over pancakes and waffles. Flavor is more distinctive than corn syrup.

HONEY
Clear honey is runny and melts better than opaque, firmly set honey. Flavor is a matter of personal choice, determined by the type of nectar the bees use.

RAISING & SETTING AGENTS

INSTANT YEAST
A powder that mixes directly into flour. Quicker and more convenient to use than other types of yeast.

BAKING POWDER
Leavening agent used in cakes and cookies. A mixture of baking soda, sodium, and cream of tartar.

BAKING SODA
Used as a leavener combined with an acid such as sour milk.

GELATIN POWDER
A setting agent that must be dissolved in liquid before use. Envelopes are most convenient. Not for vegetarians.

INSTANT YEAST

BAKING SODA

BAKING POWDER

GELATIN POWDER

FLAVORINGS

EXTRACTS
For best flavor, always buy pure extracts, not synthetic ones. Vanilla and almond are most useful.

CHOCOLATE
For the most chocolatey flavor, buy good-quality chocolate with a minimum of 70 percent cocoa solids.

COCOA POWDER
Instant chocolate flavor for cakes, sauces, and desserts. Saves melting.

VANILLA BEANS
For infusing custards with pure vanilla flavor. Split lengthwise before use. Can be stored in a jar of sugar to make vanilla sugar.

VANILLA EXTRACT   ALMOND EXTRACT

VANILLA BEANS

CHOCOLATE   COCOA POWDER

BUY THE BEST EQUIPMENT you can afford – it is false economy to save money at the outset because cheap equipment simply will not last. Good equipment will make preparation of ingredients and cooking easier for you, and it will also save you time. Think hard about the equipment you will need to start with, and buy the bare minimum. Then collect more pieces as and when you need them, gradually building up a useful assortment. This will spread the cost and prevent your kitchen cabinet and work surfaces from being cluttered with things you don't use.

EQUIPMENT

KNIVES & GADGETS

A selection of carefully chosen knives is essential in the kitchen.

Gadgets are useful but take up valuable storage space, so

buy as the need arises and build up a set that suits your cooking style.

KNIVES

BUY GOOD-QUALITY knives and keep them in a block or on a wall-mounted magnetic strip. Knives kept in a drawer get blunt quickly and are a danger to fingers.

SERRATED KNIFE
This 3in (7cm) knife blade is for slicing, especially vegetables such as tomatoes that are firm outside and soft inside.

PARING KNIFE
A knife for fine work, such as peeling (paring), cutting cores from apple quarters and peppers. The blade is 4in (10cm) long.

CHEF'S KNIFE
All-purpose chopping knife with an 8in (20cm) blade: keep the tip on the board and rock the handle up and down, moving the blade across the food.

BREAD KNIFE
Serrated knife with a 8½in (22cm) blade will cut bread crusts cleanly. These knives cannot be sharpened.

SAFETY PRONG

CARVING FORK
Holds the meat firmly. Safety prong prevents the knife blade from slipping toward the carver.

CARVING KNIFE
This 8in (20cm), thin, flexible blade carves meat in thin slices. Knife should curve upward toward the tip.

SHARPENING STEEL
To keep knives sharp, draw the blade lightly down the steel at a shallow angle. Repeat several times to the front and back of the steel.

SAFETY GUARD

BOARDS
Wooden boards are kindest to knives. Keep different boards for different purposes so there is no possibility of raw food contaminating cooked food. Clean thoroughly after use.

KNIFE SHARPENER
Easier for the beginner to use than a steel. Draw the blade backward through the sharpener several times, keeping the knife upright.

SWIVEL PEELER
The handle of this peeler is easy to grip, and the rocking blade slides over the contours of the most uneven vegetable. The hardened steel blade will stay sharp but can rust, so dry well after washing.

CAN OPENER
A sturdy, well-made can opener will work easily and leave no dangerous jagged edges. Look for cutting wheels like these and handles that are comfortable to hold.

APPLE CORER
Comes into its own when stuffing apples for baking, or making apple rings when you want to keep apples whole but remove the cores cleanly.

SKEWERS
Use a flat-bladed skewer so that when you turn a kebab over the food will turn with it.

LARGE NARROW SPATULA
This knife is used for spreading, not cutting, and has a flat, blunt, highly flexible 8½in (22cm) blade. Use it to coat a cake evenly with jam or icing, or to layer white sauce in lasagne.

ZESTER
Use to get pure strips of citrus zest (oil-rich rind with no white pith). Choose a sturdy one with a comfortable handle – you will have to grip quite hard to get the required result.

CORKSCREW
This corkscrew is easier to use than most other kinds; it requires only a single action to withdraw the cork.

SCISSORS
Keep a pair solely for kitchen use. They are perfect for snipping herbs and other small tasks.

BOTTLE STOPPER
Preserves wine or soft drinks once the bottle has been opened.

SMALL NARROW SPATULA
This smaller version is also good for spreading or for loosening a cake from its pan.

BOTTLE OPENER
Choose a simple, sturdy bottle opener with a handle that is easy to grip.

LASER

PROCESSING TOOLS

It is essential to use the right tool for the job – a cliché, but

a concept that is very important in the kitchen. The

wrong tools will only cause frustration and waste valuable time.

PROCESSING BY HAND

GOOD INGREDIENTS deserve good treatment. Having the right tools means wasting less of the food you buy. Here are the basic items that every cook should have.

BOX GRATER
Better than a flat grater because it stands up. Remember to shake grated ingredients out before they get too compressed. Two grating surfaces (large and small holes) suffice.

POTATO MASHER
It takes effort to mash potatoes, so choose a masher with a comfortable handle, such as this rubber one.

PEPPER & SALT MILLS
Freshly ground pepper is a must. Pepper loses its aroma soon after crushing, so pre-ground is a bad buy. The salt mill makes up the pair; it uses large crystals of sea salt.

NUTMEG GRATER
As with pepper, so with nutmeg – always grind your own as and when you need it. There is a compartment in the top to store the whole nutmeg.

LEMON SQUEEZER
This rigid plastic squeezer has a bowl to catch all the lemon juice and a tight-fitting strainer to keep the seeds out.

MORTAR & PESTLE
Buy the biggest one you can easily store. Porcelain is a good choice as it has the weight of marble without the prohibitive cost.

DETACHABLE GRILL

GARLIC PRESS
Choose a sturdy, all-metal press with a detachable grill to make cleaning easy.

24

PROCESSING BY MACHINE

EQUIPPING YOUR KITCHEN with the full range of small appliances is costly and wastes storage space. When buying, think carefully about what you cook, how often, and the quantities involved.

SLICING DISK

SHREDDING DISK

FINE-GRATING DISK

FRENCH FRY DISK

HANDHELD MIXER
Much faster than whisking and mixing by hand. Leaves you with one hand free and can be used in a pot over the heat. Choose one with three speeds and beaters that are easy to remove for cleaning.

BLENDER
Use to purée foods for soups, dips, batters, and drinks. Look for a model with blades set low to handle small quantities.

FOOD PROCESSOR
Eliminates the need for a freestanding blender. The metal blade chops and mixes; attachment disks shred and grate. The more expensive the processor, the more sophisticated the jobs it will do. Some come with a mini bowl for processing small quantities.

MINI BOWL

HANDHELD BLENDER
Use to purée foods in the pot. Less expensive, more portable version of the blender; it saves on cleanup and storage space. An item for small quantities – it may be all you need.

MEASURING & MIXING

Never underestimate the need for accurate measurements,

especially when baking. Using the right tools for

sifting and mixing ingredients is critical for the end result, too.

MEASURING

BUYING AND USING good measuring equipment will always pay off, especially when it comes to baking pies, bread, or cakes, when accuracy is so important for successful results.

MEASURING CUP
Buy a two- or four-cup model; a large cup is more versatile. Use glass or plastic for liquids. Plastic is safer and longer-lasting than glass, but glass is better for hot liquids. A good cup will have both US and metric measurements.

CUPS
In most recipes, solids and liquids are both measured by volume. The standard measure is the cup, which holds 8oz (250ml). Shown here are 1 cup, ½ cup, ⅓ cup, and ¼ cup dry measures.

MIXING & SIEVING

THE WOODEN SPOON is often used as a symbol of good home cooking. Certainly it does plenty of work, but the spatula and the angled spoon are probably more versatile.

SPOONS
When a recipe calls for teaspoons and tablespoons, these should be level – and measured accurately. Invest in a metal set; ordinary spoons are not accurate enough.

SCALES
Scales can be useful for weighing meat, as well as vegetables and fruit for preserving. Balance scales such as these give the most accurate results, especially for small amounts.

WOODEN SPOONS
A short-handled wooden spoon is useful for mixing and beating by hand. Long-handled spoons are good for stirring mixtures on the stove. They stand up to the heat (without burning your hand) and do not scratch the pan. A spoon with a corner will reach right to the edges at the bottom of a pan.

COLANDER

SIEVES
It is handy to have two: large and small. Besides sifting dry ingredients and straining wet ones, you can use a sieve to purée cooked fruit and vegetables, and to make puréed soups.

LADLE

SERVING SPOON

SLOTTED SPOON

SPATULA

COLANDER
Choose a freestanding, sturdy colander with handles for safe draining of cooked vegetables, pasta, and beans.

BOWLS

BOWLS
Useful to have plenty of sizes, but choose ones that fit inside one another so that they do not take up all your storage space. Glass is versatile, and gives you an all-around view of what you are mixing.

KITCHEN TOOL SET
Ladle *To avoid pouring hot liquids from heavy pans, use this for serving soups and stews.*

Serving spoon *The handle gets hot if this spoon is left in the pan, so use for serving only.*

Spatula *For any solid food that needs turning in the pan or lifting carefully from pan to plate. It is especially useful for delicate foods like fish that have a tendency to break up.*

Slotted spoon *Invaluable when removing food from boiling water for serving or testing, and for skimming scum from the surface of liquids. Can be either round or spoon-shaped.*

WOODEN SPATULA
This flat-sided spatula is used for folding mixtures, like egg whites or melted chocolate and cake mixture, together. It doubles as a lifter and turner, too.

BALLOON WHISK
A comfortable handle and a large balloon of springy wire will make light work of whisking egg whites if you don't have an electric mixer. A good tool to use whenever you need to incorporate air into a mixture.

COIL WHISK
Ideal for whisking small quantities of sauce in a saucepan or roasting pan – but do not use on nonstick finishes.

FLEXIBLE SPATULA
A flexible plastic or rubber spatula is the best way to make sure you get every last bit of mixture out of the bowl. Like a wooden spatula, it is good for folding mixtures, too.

TONGS
Useful for turning and moving delicate pieces of hot food, especially when barbecuing.

PASTRY TOOLS

PASTRY-MAKING IS A PRECISE ART, and you will need some special tools besides cold hands if you are going to be successful. You can either make the pastry on a board (see page 22) or work directly on a floured work surface – marble is ideal because it stays cool.

PASTRY BRUSH
Use for sealing and glazing. This is the flat, paintbrush kind – easier to use than the round type.

PIE FUNNEL
Holds up the pastry lid and pokes through the top so that steam can escape and the pastry stays crisp.

COOKIE CUTTERS
Available plain and fluted as shown here, and also in a wide range of shapes and sizes, from letters of the alphabet to hearts and stars.

WOODEN ROLLING PIN
Choose a heavy, smooth rolling pin without handles. The best way to roll pastry is to roll the whole pin under the palms, sliding the hands up and down to distribute the weight evenly – handles are not necessary.

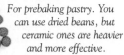

PIE WEIGHTS
For prebaking pastry. You can use dried beans, but ceramic ones are heavier and more effective.

POTS & PANS

Pots and pans are perhaps the most important pieces of equipment in your kitchen, so buy the best you can afford. Choose quality pans – they will last for years, and save wasted time and burned food.

CHOOSING POTS & PANS

YOU NEED A MINIMUM of three deep pots and one shallow pan. A sauté pan is the most versatile of the shallow pans. Unless otherwise stated, measurements are taken across the top.

STEAMER BASKET
A collapsible steamer basket stands on metal legs inside the pan. It can be folded up when not in use and is less expensive than a regular steamer.

LARGE POT
Like the medium pot, this 8½in (22cm) pot doubles as a casserole. It holds about 5 quarts and can accommodate a steamer basket.

MEDIUM POT
This 7in (18cm) two-handled pot can be used on the stove and in the oven: its two short metal handles allow it to fit in the oven like a casserole dish. It holds about 3 quarts, a useful size for most cooking purposes, and comes with a tight-fitting lid.

SAUCEPAN
This 6¼in (16cm) multifunctional pan holds about 2 quarts. Use it to make sauces, vegetables, soups, and small stews. A long handle will stay cooler on a hot stovetop.

SMALL SAUCEPAN
Holds about 1 quart of liquid. Nonstick is best for sauces with milk or cream in them because they have a tendency to stick. A pouring lip on both sides makes serving easier. Nonstick finishes vary widely and never last forever; the better the quality, the more durable they will be.

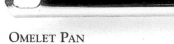

OMELET PAN
A pan with a nonstick finish is easiest to use. The right size is important: measuring across the base, use a 6¼in (16cm) pan for a two-egg French omelet, a 9in (23cm) pan for a thick Spanish or Italian omelet. These pans are also useful for making pancakes.

WOK

Choose a large wok, 13½in (35cm), if you have room to store it. Preseasoned carbon steel is easy to care for and can take metal implements; unseasoned carbon steel rusts more easily. A wok with a slightly flattened bottom is most stable on both gas and electric burners. Woks often come complete with ladle, spatula, and shovel.

SPATULA

SHOVEL

LADLE

WOK LID

SAUTÉ PAN

A good-quality, nonstick 8in (20cm) sauté pan will prove useful for shallow frying as well as boiling or stir-frying. A sauté pan has deeper, straighter sides than a frying pan. This one has a removable handle, which, like the short-handled pans on the facing page, allows for oven use. The glass lid enables you to see what is happening when you cover the pan.

STOVETOP GRILL

Stovetop grilling is an easy way to achieve a professional-looking result at home. Choose a pan with defined ridges, and check that it is not so heavy that you cannot easily lift it. A foldaway handle is useful for easy storage.

CHOICE OF MATERIALS FOR POTS & PANS

STAINLESS STEEL IS THE BEST ALL-AROUND CHOICE; it's extremely durable and easy to clean. For the best heat conduction, buy good-quality pots and pans that have heavy bases made of a sandwich of stainless steel with a metal filling. Good conductors of heat are copper, copper and silver alloy, or aluminum, so look for a filling made of one of these. Although expensive, a good pot or pan should last a very long time.

BAKING & ROASTING

Equipment for baking and roasting is probably not used every day, so
you need not spend a fortune. However, avoid anything flimsy.
Pans that bend in your hands may cast your handiwork on the floor.

OVENWARE

THE CHOICE OF METAL or
ceramic, nonstick or
uncoated, depends
largely on the job you
want the equipment
to do. Whatever you
buy, take good care of
it to avoid rusting
and scratching.

LAYER CAKE PAN
*This loose-bottomed cake pan is
8in (20cm) in diameter and
shallow. You will need two to
make a layer cake, but you
may want to invest in
more if you make a lot of
small cakes. A nonstick
coating is not necessary.*

RAMEKINS
*Ramekins – small ceramic baking
dishes – are for individual servings
of soufflés and baked custards, and
can be brought straight to the table
from the oven. The average capacity
is ¾ cup (about 150ml).*

MUFFIN TIN

MUFFIN TIN
*A nonstick coating is extremely
useful in a muffin tin. If the pan is
not nonstick, use paper liners, or
grease the cups well.*

BAKING SHEET
*Buy the largest one that will fit
comfortably in your oven. It should
be sturdy, inflexible, and completely
flat. Use it for pizzas and cookies,
and to provide a heat-conducting
base for quiches, pies, and tarts.*

COOLING RACK
*Cakes should always be cooled before
being filled, sandwiched together, or
iced, and a metal cooling rack allows
air to circulate around them.*

COOLING RACK

SPRINGFORM PAN
*This one is 8in (20cm) in
diameter. The clasp on the
side opens the pan and
releases the bottom, so a
cake can be removed
easily. Use a pan of this
size and style for delicate
cakes and cheesecakes
that break up easily.
Nonstick is not necessary.
A cake pan needs to be
lined and greased for a good
result regardless of the material
it is made from or its coating.*

**SHEET
CAKE PAN**
*Select a deep-sided tray
measuring about
9 x 13in (23 x 33cm).
Take care when
cutting not to scratch
the nonstick surface.*

LOAF PAN
*A nonstick pan is the
most versatile. Use it
for bread, and also for
pâtés and terrines.*

BAKING SHEET   SHEET CAKE PAN

FAT-FREE
SPOUT

FAT
POURER

BAKING DISH
A well-made ceramic dish measuring about 8 x 10in (20 x 25cm) across the top and 2in (5cm) in depth is perfect for baked pasta dishes and can be used for roasting as well. Dishes such as these cannot usually bear sudden and extreme temperature changes: while they are fine in the oven, they must not be transferred to a stovetop. Nor should cold water be poured into a very hot dish to cool it down; it might crack.

GRAVY SEPARATOR
This gravy boat enables the diner to pour fat-free gravies and sauces. Fat floats to the surface and can be poured off through a shallow spout on some models. The deep spout reaches into the liquid below.

PIE PAN
Metal is better than ceramic or ovenproof glass for cooking pastry because it distributes the heat more evenly and gives a crisper result. A very hot baking sheet under the pie pan increases heat conduction. Pie pans have plain, sloping sides and a lip for the pie edging.

POULTRY PINS
Small pins can be used to truss poultry to hold it together while it cooks.

ROASTING PAN
Best of all is a deep, enameled pan with a pouring lip. It should be strong, rigid, and as big as your oven will take.

MEAT THERMOMETER
Use for large birds and roasts: insert the thermometer probe through the thickest part of the meat at the start of cooking. For temperatures, see page 160.

ROASTING RACK
A rack allows meat to be roasted free of its own fat. A hinged one can be folded to cradle a bird.

QUICHE PAN
As with the pie pan above, a metal quiche pan performs better than a ceramic one. Quiches are fragile, and the fluted edge helps strengthen the pastry shell. This pan measures 8in (20cm) across the base, which lifts out so the whole quiche can be removed without breaking. For easy serving, leave the quiche on the base.

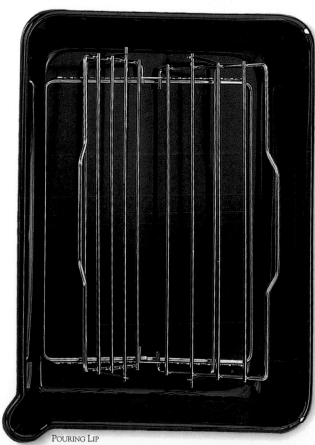

POURING LIP

USING AN OVEN

FEW NEW COOKS HAVE THE LUXURY OF CHOOSING their own oven, but whatever is available, each oven will vary in performance. Get to know your oven's capabilities and adjust cooking times and temperatures to suit your oven. Convection ovens are hotter than conventional ovens, so lower temperatures are used, but always consult the manufacturer's handbook.

GOOD BASIC COOKING SKILLS are essential for the new cook, and they're easy to master. Once you've learned them, you will never forget them, and you will be confident that you can cook well and have good results every time. In this chapter you will learn how to choose ingredients wisely and how to prepare them correctly. You will also learn basic cooking methods, the ones you will use over and over again on a daily basis. Step-by-step photographs guide you effortlessly through the cooking process, from simple skills like cracking an egg without breaking the yolk, to boiling potatoes and cooking spaghetti, to trickier tasks like stuffing and trussing a turkey.

TECHNIQUES

EGGS

Eggs are one of the most inexpensive sources of complete protein and could not be easier to cook. Once you have mastered these simple techniques, you will be able to produce a nutritious meal in minutes.

BOILING

REMOVE EGGS FROM THE REFRIGERATOR 30 minutes before cooking: if they are very cold, they will crack in hot water. Times given here are for large eggs. For safety information on soft-boiled eggs, see page 162.

SOFT BOILING

Using a slotted spoon, gently lower the egg into a small saucepan two thirds full of simmering water. Bring to a boil, lower the heat to a gentle simmer, and set a timer for 4 minutes. When the time is up, remove the egg with a slotted spoon and slice across the top with a knife. The egg will have a runny yolk.

HARD BOILING

Follow the instructions for soft boiling, but simmer the egg for 10 minutes. Do not cook longer or a black ring will form around the yolk. Lift the egg out with a slotted spoon and plunge it into a bowl of cold water. Crack the shell and peel it off. Immerse the egg in cold water for at least 5 minutes until cool.

CRACKING AN EGG

THERE IS NO SPECIAL TRICK to prevent egg yolks from breaking when you crack open the shell, so always crack each egg into an empty bowl.

Tap the middle of the egg sharply against the rim of a small bowl. Holding the egg low over the bowl, insert the tips of your thumbs into the crack in the shell and gently pry the shell apart. Tip the contents of the egg into the bowl and discard the shell. Remove any pieces of shell with the tip of a teaspoon.

FRYING

ALWAYS ENSURE that the fat is hot before adding the egg. If you like a yolk with a film of white on top, continue spooning the fat over it in step 2 until it is opaque. For safety information on runny yolks, see page 162.

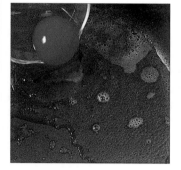

1 Heat 1½ tsp each sunflower oil and butter in a sauté pan until foaming. Slide the egg from a bowl into the pan.

2 Fry over medium heat for 3–4 minutes, until the white is set, spooning the fat over the yolk to help it cook.

3 Lift the egg out with a spatula and let the fat drain back into the pan. If frying more than 1 egg, cut the whites apart with the spatula first.

POACHING

USE EITHER A NONSTICK small saucepan or sauté pan. Fill the pan two thirds full with water and bring to a boil, then add a pinch of salt. Turn the heat down so the water is simmering gently before adding the eggs: rapidly boiling water will break up the whites. A nonstick egg poacher that cooks eggs in butter can also be used. For safety information on lightly poached eggs, see page 162.

1 Slide the egg from a bowl into gently simmering salted water. Turn the heat down to low.

2 Poach, uncovered, over low heat for about 3 minutes, until the white is opaque and the yolk is runny.

3 Lift the egg out with a slotted spoon and let the excess water drain back into the pan.

SCRAMBLING

EGGS ARE BEST SCRAMBLED in a nonstick small saucepan or sauté pan, so they do not stick and burn on the bottom. For creamy scrambled eggs, the secret is to cook the eggs very gently and slowly, stirring all the time. Serve plain or with chopped fresh herbs. For a special occasion, replace the milk with cream and serve the eggs scattered with thin strips of smoked salmon.

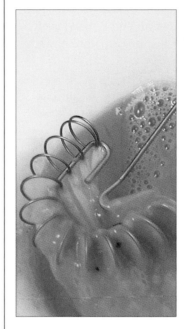 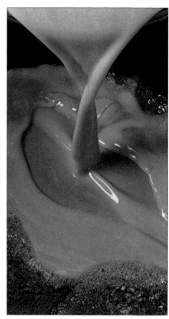

1 For each person, whisk together 2 eggs, 1 tbsp milk, and a little salt and pepper.

2 Heat 1 tbsp butter in the pan until foaming, then pour in the egg mixture.

3 Cook over low heat, stirring gently with a wooden spatula. When almost set, remove from the heat, stir for 1 more minute, then serve at once.

EGGS

SEPARATING EGGS

IF YOU NEED EGG WHITES for soufflés or meringues, or yolks for mayonnaise, you must separate the whites from the yolks before you start. For 1 egg, use two bowls: one for the white and one for the yolk. If separating more eggs, use three bowls and separate over an empty bowl each time, tipping the whites and yolks into separate bowls.

Tap the middle of the egg sharply against the rim of a small bowl. Hold the egg low over the bowl and pry the shell apart with the tips of your thumbs. Tilt gently to pour the white into the bowl while retaining the yolk in the shell. Tip the yolk from the shell into the second bowl.

BEATING EGG WHITES

YOU WILL GET a greater volume when beating egg whites if they are at room temperature rather than cold, so take them out of the refrigerator 30 minutes before needed. Equipment must be scrupulously clean and dry.

1 Place the egg whites in a large bowl. Using an electric mixer on full speed, begin beating, moving the beaters around the bowl.

2 Continue beating on full speed, still moving the beaters around the bowl, until the egg whites stand in stiff peaks. Use at once.

MAKING MERINGUES

THIS RECIPE makes 12 meringues. They are usually sandwiched in pairs. For serving ideas, see page 152.

INGREDIENTS

2 egg whites

½ cup (110g) superfine sugar

1 Preheat the oven to 275°F (140°C). Beat the whites until stiff (see left), then add the sugar 1 tsp at a time, beating on full speed until glossy.

2 Cover a baking sheet with a piece of waxed paper. Place 12 individual spoonfuls of the mixture onto the paper, swirling them with the back of the spoon.

3 Bake for ¾–1 hour, until firm and crisp. Lift one to check that it comes easily off the paper. Let the meringues cool slightly, then lift them off with a spatula.

Making Crepe Batter

VERY THIN PANCAKES, called *crêpes* in French, are quite tricky to make because they tend to stick and tear, so it is easier to make fewer, thicker pancakes the first few times you try. It is not essential to let the batter stand.

Ingredients

1 cup (125g) all-purpose flour
2 eggs
1 cup (250ml) milk, either whole or low-fat

 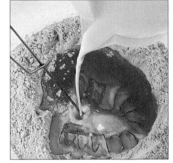

1 Measure the flour into a bowl, make a well in the center, and add the eggs. Whisk, drawing in the flour.

2 Continue whisking, pouring in the milk a little at a time and gradually drawing in all the flour.

3 Whisk until smooth. Let stand for about 30 minutes, so the starch grains absorb liquid and swell.

Cooking Crepes

DEPENDING ON PANCAKE SIZE required, use a 6¼in (16cm) or 8–9in (20–23cm) pan: a nonstick omelet pan is ideal. Heat over medium heat for 1–2 minutes, then wipe it with a wad of paper towels dipped in sunflower oil.

1 Ladle enough batter into the greased hot pan to cover the bottom, tilting the pan so that it spreads evenly.

2 Cook over medium heat for 60 seconds, or until golden underneath. Loosen the edge and flip the pancake over.

3 Cook the other side of the pancake for 30 seconds, or until golden. Slide onto a plate. Reheat the pan and oil it again before making the next pancake. A 6¼in (16cm) pan will make twelve pancakes; a 9in (23cm) pan will make eight.

RICE & PASTA

It is essential to know how to cook rice and pasta well: they provide

vital carbohydrates, and are the basis for a huge variety of dishes.

The methods shown here are easy to follow – and almost foolproof.

─COOKING RICE─

THE ABSORPTION METHOD shown here is best, especially for long-grain and basmati rice, and a measuring cup is the easiest and most accurate way to gauge quantities.

1 To serve four people, pour 1 cup (300ml) rice into a medium pot. Measure 2 cups (600ml) water in the same measuring cup.

2 Add the water to the rice, then add 1 tsp salt and bring to a boil over medium heat. Stir once, then lower the heat to a gentle simmer.

3 Cover the pot tightly and cook gently for the time stated (see right). Keep covered during cooking.

─TESTING & SERVING RICE─

COOKING TIMES VARY, so check the package first. As a general rule, cook white long-grain rice 12–15 minutes, brown rice 20–30 minutes, basmati rice 10–15 minutes.

1 At the end of the cooking time, lift the lid and check that the top of the rice is dry. Tilt the pot to see if all the water has been absorbed.

2 Cook for a little longer if there is still some water left. When all the water is gone, the rice will be tender and the grains separate.

3 Remove the pot from the heat. Let stand, covered, for 5 minutes. Before serving, fluff up the rice with a fork.

COOKING PASTA

FOR FOUR PEOPLE, allow 4 quarts (4 liters) water, 1 tbsp salt, and ¾lb (400g) dried pasta/1lb (500g) fresh pasta. Most dried shapes cook in 10–15 minutes, fresh in 2–3 minutes, but check the package and test for doneness just before the recommended time. Shapes like penne, gnocchi, and conchiglie trap water, so drain these well.

COOKING SPAGHETTI

THIS LONG PASTA is cooked in the same way as any other pasta (see left), but it requires a little extra care at the beginning – even the shorter lengths of spaghetti are unlikely to fit into your pot without softening first. Fresh spaghetti is an exception because it is soft; it cooks very quickly – check the package for exact time.

1 Bring the water to a boil in a large pot. Add the salt, then the pasta, and bring back to a boil. Set a timer for the recommended time.

2 Cook, uncovered, over high heat. Stir often with a slotted spoon during cooking to keep the shapes from sticking to one another.

1 Bring the water to a boil in a large pot. Add the salt after the water has started to boil, then lower one end of the spaghetti into the water.

2 As the spaghetti softens, coil it into the water until it is submerged. Start timing from this moment, and stir often to keep the strands separate.

NOODLES

DRIED CHINESE EGG NOODLES come conveniently packed in flat sheets. Three sheets, weighing ½lb (250g) in total, are enough for four people. Cooking methods differ from one brand to another, but this is one of the quickest and most efficient ways to prepare them.

3 Just before the time is up, lift out some pasta and pinch it with your fingers, or bite into it. It should be tender, but retain some bite (*al dente*).

4 Remove the pot from the heat and drain the pasta in a large colander. Shake the colander vigorously to drain off as much water as possible.

1 Bring plenty of water to a boil in a large pot. Add the noodles and stir to separate them. Remove the pot from the heat.

2 Cover the pot and let stand for 6 minutes. Drain the noodles thoroughly in a colander. Toss noodles with 1–2 tsp sesame oil, if you like.

GRAINS & LEGUMES

The combination of grains and legumes is nature's power-pack.

When eaten together they provide a complete source of protein:

low in fat, high in vitamins, minerals, and fiber, and tasty too.

BULGUR WHEAT

ALSO KNOWN AS BURGHUL, this is wheat that has been precooked, dried, and crushed. It is extremely quick and simple to prepare – it only needs to be soaked before use. For four people you will need about ¾ cup (100g) bulgur: serve it warm in pilafs or cold in salads like tabbouleh.

1 Put the bulgur in a large bowl. Add enough cold water to cover it generously. Let stand for 20–30 minutes.

2 Tip the bulgur into a sieve and squeeze it with your hands to remove as much excess water as possible.

COUSCOUS

COUSCOUS IS A PRECOOKED product made from wheat. Traditionally, Moroccans steam it in a special pan over a meat or vegetable stew, but a quick alternative is shown here. To serve four, use 1½ cups (400ml) water, 1 tsp salt, 1 tbsp olive oil, and 1½ cups (250g) couscous.

1 Bring the water to a boil in a medium pot. Add the salt, oil, and couscous. Remove from the heat, stir, and cover.

2 Let stand for 5 minutes, return to the stove and cook over medium heat, stirring with a fork, for 3–5 minutes.

POLENTA

BOILED POLENTA IS GOOD with meat, poultry, and casseroles with lots of sauce. Instructions are given here for instant polenta, which is easier to cook than ordinary polenta. For four people, use 4½ cups (1 liter) water, 1 tsp salt, 2 cups (250g) polenta, and 3 tbsp butter.

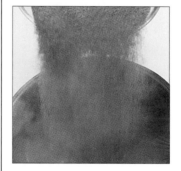

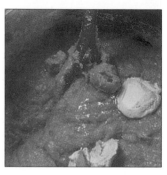

1 Bring the water to a boil in a large pot. Add the salt, then pour in the polenta in a steady stream.

2 Cook over very low heat, stirring constantly, until it pulls away from the pot, about 8 minutes. Add the butter.

3 Remove from the heat and beat until the polenta holds its shape. Check seasoning.

LENTILS

FOR THE BUSY COOK, lentils are invaluable because, unlike other beans, they do not need soaking – and they cook in little time. Red and orange lentils cook to a soft, mushy consistency and are often served as a side dish or in Indian dhal; green, Puy, and brown lentils hold their shape and are good in salads. For all types, use 1¼ cups (250g) lentils and 2½ cups (600ml) water to serve four.

DRIED BEANS & PEAS

ALL DRIED BEANS EXCEPT LENTILS need soaking overnight, then boiling rapidly for 10 minutes. Cooking times range from 45 minutes for adzuki beans to 2 hours for chickpeas; most beans take 1–1½ hours. For precise times, see page 161, and check the package. Skim off any scum that forms during cooking with a slotted spoon. Once cooked, drain and use in salads, purées, and stews.

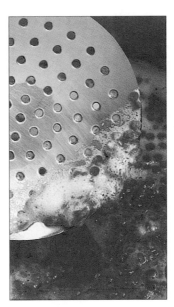

1 Rinse the lentils in a sieve under cold running water, then put them in a pot with the water. Bring to a boil.

2 Skim off the scum with a slotted spoon. Cook, uncovered, over medium heat for 20–30 minutes.

1 Put beans or peas in a large bowl and cover generously with cold water. Let soak for at least 8 hours. Drain and rinse.

2 Put the beans or peas in a pot; cover generously with cold water. Bring to a boil and boil rapidly for 10 minutes.

3 Check that all the water has been absorbed and the lentils are tender. Add salt to taste.

3 Reduce the heat to low, cover, and simmer gently until tender. To test, squeeze gently – they should feel soft through to the center.

FISH

Fish is nutritious, low in fat, and quick to cook. At the supermarket

and fishmonger it is sold gutted and scaled, and often

cut into serving portions, so very little preparation is needed.

—BUYING—

WHEN CHOOSING FISH, look for firm, moist flesh, and ask for it to be cut while you wait. All the fish shown here are easy to find, prepare, and cook. A whole fish weighing ¾–1lb (350–500g) is enough for one person; for fillets, allow about ¼lb (125g) per person.

Sole fillets *for pan-frying and broiling. Treat flounder fillets in the same way.*

Whole trout *for baking, broiling, and poaching. Try sea bass and mullet too.*

Salmon fillets *for broiling, grilling, pan-frying, and baking. Sea bass fillets can be cooked like this too.*

Cod steak *for pan-frying, broiling, poaching, and baking. Salmon steaks can be cooked in the same way.*

Haddock fillet *for broiling, pan-frying, and baking. Cook cod and hake fillets the same way.*

—PREPARING A WHOLE FISH—

THIS IS ONE OF THE BEST WAYS TO PREPARE a whole fish for broiling or baking. The trimming of the fins and tail gives the fish a neat, attractive appearance, and lemon slices and herbs impart flavor to the flesh. For extra moistness, brush skin with olive oil before cooking.

1 Using kitchen scissors, cut all the fins off the back and the stomach of the fish. Discard the fins.

2 Cut the tail into a neat "V" shape. Rinse the fish under cold running water, then pat thoroughly dry.

3 Using a chef's knife, make several diagonal slashes in each side of the fish, cutting right down to the bone.

4 Insert a few sprigs of fresh parsley and a lemon slice in each slash, then sprinkle the fish with salt and pepper.

PREPARING FILLETS

INDIVIDUAL FILLETS ARE CONVENIENT because they cook very quickly. Salmon is shown here, but haddock, hake, sea bass, and cod can be prepared in the same way. Fish is sometimes sold in a long piece, which is one side of the fish after it has been filleted – this will need to be cut into individual servings of about ¼lb (125g). One of the quickest and tastiest ways to cook salmon fillets is by grilling – see the Master Recipe on page 92.

1 Run your fingertips along the flesh to feel for tiny pin bones. Pull out with a pair of tweezers or with your fingers.

2 Using a chef's knife, trim any ragged skin or fat from the edges of the fillet so you are left with a neat shape.

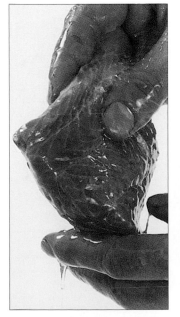

3 Rinse for a few seconds under cold running water, rubbing the skin with your fingers to dislodge any scales.

4 Lay the fillets skin side down on paper towels. Pat them dry with more paper towels before cooking.

SKINNING FILLETS

A FISHMONGER WILL REMOVE the skin from fish fillets if asked, but most packaged fish from supermarkets comes with the skin on. It can be cooked like this, and the skin will help hold the flesh together, but you may prefer to remove it. If the fish is to be coated before cooking, the skin must be removed. Fish fillets are slippery, so dip your fingers in salt to get a firm grip on the fish before skinning. Use a chef's knife to cut.

1 Skin side down, grip the tail end of the fish between salted index finger and thumb.

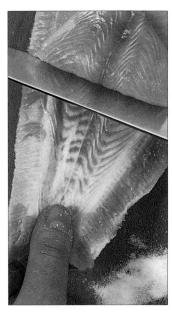

2 Working away from you with a sawing action, cut between the skin and flesh.

COATING FILLETS

EGG AND BREAD CRUMBS make a crunchy coating and protect fish during cooking. For 4 fillets, use 1 large egg and 1 cup (75g) fresh or dried bread crumbs (see page 70). Make sure the fish is absolutely dry, and sprinkle the crumbs on a sheet of waxed paper before you start.

1 Beat the egg in a shallow dish. Dip the fillet in the egg, turn it to coat, then lift it up to drain off the excess egg.

2 Transfer the fillet to the bread crumbs. Lift the sides of the paper and shake the crumbs over the fish to coat.

SHELLFISH

A good source of low-fat protein, fresh and frozen shellfish are now available in most supermarkets. If you follow the simple techniques shown here, you will find they are easy to prepare and cook.

BUYING

GENERALLY SPEAKING, IT IS BEST to buy raw shellfish and cook it yourself. It will taste fresher and have juicier flesh than shellfish that is bought ready-cooked. Fresh mussels and clams are generally sold raw and alive in their shells; if they are shelled they are stored in brine.

Tiger prawns, *raw (top) and cooked. For broiling, stir-frying, and pan-frying.*

Scallop *with orange coral in shell. For stir-frying, pan-frying, and broiling.*

Shrimp with heads removed, *raw (left) and cooked. For stir-frying and pan-frying.*

Mussels *small for stews and soups; large for steaming, broiling, and baking.*

Cooked shrimp in their shells *for eating cold, and in salads and stir-fries.*

Small clams *for soups and stews include the Little Neck and butter clam.*

Peeled cooked shrimp *for eating cold, and in salads, soups, and stir-fries.*

Large quahog clams *for steaming, baking, stuffings, and chowders.*

MUSSELS

ANY MUSSELS THAT HAVE BROKEN SHELLS, or open shells that do not close when tapped hard on the work surface, will be dead. Discard them. Always cook mussels on the day of purchase. To cook them, see the recipe on page 127. Buy about 4lb (2kg) mussels to serve four people.

1 Detach and discard the stringy "beard" from the shell by pulling it away with the help of a paring knife.

2 With the back of the same knife, scrape any barnacles off the mussels, always working away from you.

3 Use a small stiff brush to scrub each mussel under cold running water. This will dislodge sand from crevices in the shell, together with any remaining pieces of barnacle.

SCALLOPS

SHELLED SCALLOPS are the most commonly available. They should have a sweet, fresh smell and plump, creamy flesh. Often the orange coral is still attached – this is the roe, which is edible and looks attractive when sliced and cooked with the white meat. Whichever cooking method you choose, all scallops cook in 3–4 minutes at the most, so do not exceed this time or they will become rubbery. Allow 3–4 large scallops, or 10 bay scallops, per person.

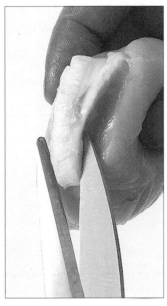
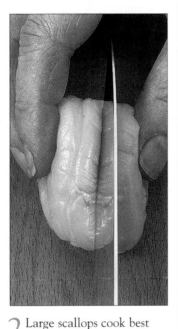

1 Using kitchen scissors, cut off the crescent-shaped muscle on the side of the white body. Discard it because it is tough and chewy.

2 Large scallops cook best if sliced. Using a chef's knife, slice through into rounds. Small bay scallops can be left whole.

CLAMS

AFTER CLEANING, steam clams in a covered pan for about 5 minutes until they are fully open. They are then ready to eat, or may be used in soups and stews. Allow ¾–1lb (375–500g) small clams or 2–3 quahogs per person.

Live clams in their shells must be cleaned before cooking. Start by soaking them for at least 1 hour in cold salted water (4 tbsp salt to 4½ cups/1 liter water) – this will help dislodge some of the sand. After soaking, drain the clams and scrub them hard with a stiff brush under cold running water to remove any remaining sand and grit (unlike mussels, there is no stringy "beard"). As you work, discard any open clams or clams with broken shells.

SHRIMP

IN THEIR RAW STATE, shrimp are gray; it is only when they are cooked that they turn the more familiar pink. Whether raw or cooked, the shell is removed in the same way. The dark vein that runs through a shrimp is edible, but it is unsightly and can be gritty in large shrimp. Remove as shown below. Allow about 10 jumbo shrimp per person, about ½lb (200g) shrimp in their shells per person, or ¼lb (125g) peeled cooked shrimp.

1 If the head is still on the shrimp, pinch it between your fingers and pull it from the body to leave just the fleshy tail end intact.

2 Peel the shell from the body with your fingers, working down from the head. When you reach the tail, pull the meat out of the shell.

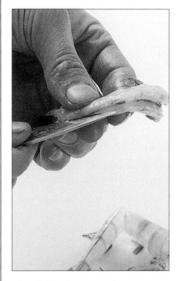
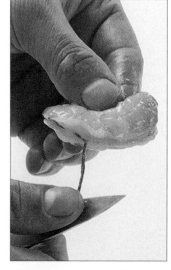

3 If the shrimp is large, remove the dark vein: make a shallow cut along the back of the shrimp with a paring knife to reveal it.

4 Pick out the end of the vein with the tip of the knife; gently pull it out, starting from the head end. Discard the vein.

45

POULTRY

Inexpensive and quick-cooking, poultry requires very little in the
way of preparation and marries well with other flavors. Most is low in
fat and even the newest cook can achieve consistently good results.

BIRDS FOR ROASTING

THERE IS A WIDE CHOICE of birds for roasting. Free-range
birds generally have the best flavor; corn-fed have a good
color, but are not always free-range. Frozen birds are good
value, and less expensive than fresh. For defrosting times
and roasting temperatures and times, see page 160.

Chicken *should have
light, moist skin and a
plump breast. 3–3½lb
(1.5–1.8kg) serves 3–4;
5–6lb (2.5–3kg) serves 6–8.*

Duck *should have
supple, waxy skin and
a long, slender breast.
3lb (1.5kg) serves 2;
5–6lb (2.5–3kg) serves 4.*

Turkey
*should have
plump legs
and breast.
9–10lb (4–5kg)
serves 8–10; 13–18lb
(6–8kg) serves 12–14.
Buy larger than you need:
roast turkey is excellent cold.*

CUTS OF POULTRY

INDIVIDUAL PIECES OF POULTRY cook much quicker than
whole birds, and make portion control easier. They
require little preparation and are extremely versatile.
For each person allow ¼lb (125g) boneless meat, a little
more if meat is on the bone.

Chicken wing with breast *for
pan-frying, broiling, and casseroles.*

Whole chicken leg *for
casseroles, pan-frying,
broiling, and roasting.*

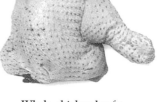

Boneless chicken breasts
*with and without skin. For
pan-frying, stir-frying, and broiling.*

Chicken livers *for
broiling, pan-frying, and
pâtés. Fresh have a better
texture than frozen.*

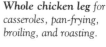

Turkey scallop (breast steak)
for pan-frying and stir-frying.

Chicken drumstick *(below left)
for broiling and barbecuing.*

Ground turkey *for
burgers: low-fat alternative
to ground beef or lamb.*

Chicken thighs *(left) with
and without skin, for baking
and barbecuing.*

Preparing a Chicken

A SMALL TO MEDIUM CHICKEN (up to 4lb/2kg) can be held together for roasting by following the steps below. Large chickens and turkeys cook better if tied (trussed) with string, especially if there is stuffing in the neck end (see page 48). If there are giblets inside the chicken, remove them before preparing the bird. For instructions on how to roast a chicken, see the Master Recipe on page 100.

Preparing Chicken Breasts

BONELESS CHICKEN BREASTS have white, low-fat meat that cooks very quickly, but they need to be cooked with care if they are to be succulent and tender. If the skin is left on, the flesh will be more moist, but the fat content will be higher. One solution is to cook the chicken with the skin on, then pull it off with your fingers just before serving.

SEPARATING THE FILLET

Pull the small strip of tender fillet away from the underside. A choice part, it takes less time to cook than the rest.

MAKING A POCKET

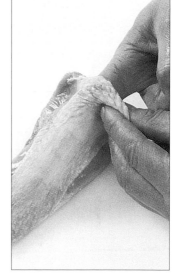

Push your finger between the skin and the flesh to make a pocket. Insert butter, soft cheese, garlic, herbs.

REMOVING THE TENDON

Strip the white tendon away from the underside of the breast using a paring knife. The tendon is sinewy and chewy; discard it.

MOISTENING THE FLESH

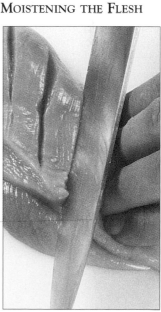

To keep skinless breasts moist, score the top on the diagonal with a chef's knife, then marinate or insert herb or garlic butter into the slits.

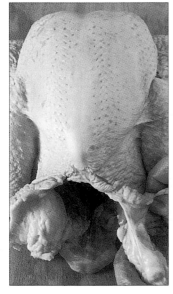

1 With your fingers, pull off the excess white fat on both sides of the opening at the tail end of the bird.

2 Wipe the cavity with paper towels, then use a fresh piece to wipe the skin. The skin crisps better if dry.

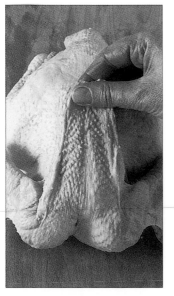

3 Turn the bird breast side down and pull the neck skin over the neck cavity. If you like, cut off the excess skin with scissors to neaten it.

4 Twist the wings around so the tips come up and over the skin to secure it. Turn the bird breast side up and tie the legs together with string.

POULTRY

—ROASTING A LARGE BIRD—

IF THE BIRD IS FROZEN, defrost it thoroughly before stuffing and cooking. If there are giblets inside, remove them. Stuff the neck end only, not the body cavity. A recipe for roast turkey is given on page 144. For defrosting times and roasting temperatures and times, see page 160.

1 Place the bird, tail end down, in a bowl. Pull neck skin back and spoon in the stuffing. Pull skin over stuffing and secure with a skewer.

2 Twist the wing tips up and over and tie with string. Pull legs in and tie with string. Spread butter over the bird and sprinkle with salt and pepper.

3 Put the bird on a rack in a roasting pan. If you have a meat thermometer, push it into the thickest part of a thigh, away from the bone.

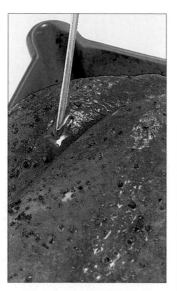

4 Roast until the juices run clear when a skewer is inserted into the thickest part of a thigh. Check temperature if using a thermometer.

—CARVING A LARGE BIRD—

LEAVE A COOKED BIRD TO REST, wrapped in foil, for about 15 minutes while making the gravy (see page 103). Unwrap, then transfer breast side up to a board. Remove trussing string and poultry pin. Steady bird with a carving fork. Use the same technique for chicken and turkey.

1 Push the wing down with the knife blade and cut through outer layer of breast into the joint. Ease wing from body; cut through the gristle.

2 Cut thin slices from one side of the breast, parallel to the rib cage and include some stuffing with each slice. Repeat on the other side.

3 Remove one leg by twisting it outward, then cutting through the joint. Hold the leg and carve slices from the thigh. Repeat with the other leg.

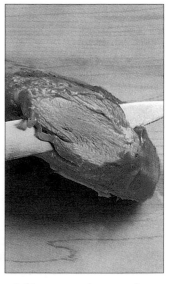

4 To remove the meat from the drumsticks, hold the knuckle bone and, working from this end, cut thin slices parallel to the bone.

ROASTING DUCK

DUCK HAS LESS EDIBLE MEAT than other birds of similar weight because it is fatty and has a large bone structure. It has a rich flavor, so portions are smaller than for chicken or turkey. Prepare it in the same way as chicken (see page 47), but remove as much visible fat as possible before you begin. This will reduce fattiness, as will pricking the breast with a fork before roasting and cooking the bird upside down at the beginning. For defrosting times and roasting temperatures and times, see page 160.

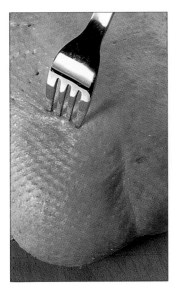

1 Prick the breast all over, then rub with salt and pepper. Place, breast side down, on a rack in a roasting pan. Roast for 25 minutes.

2 Turn breast side up and roast for 20 minutes. Baste, then pour off excess fat. Finish roasting at a lower oven temperature (see page 160).

SERVING DUCK

A DUCK IS BEST CUT into serving pieces rather than carved. To be sure that each person will get a good amount of meat, use the technique shown here for four people. For two, simply cut the duck lengthwise in half.

1 Cut away the legs by slicing through the joints with a carving knife. Cut along both sides of the breastbone to free the breast meat.

2 Cut each piece of breast on the diagonal into thick slices. Serve each person some breast meat and either a wing or a leg.

CHICKEN STOCK

KEEP STOCK COVERED in the refrigerator for 3 days, or freeze for 6 months. Makes about 4 cups (1 liter) stock.

INGREDIENTS

| 1 leftover roast chicken carcass |
| 1 medium onion, halved |
| 1 medium celery stalk, chopped |
| 1 medium carrot, chopped |
| 1 bouquet garni |

1 Break the carcass up to fit into a large pot. Add the vegetables and bouquet garni. Stir, then add cold water to cover the ingredients well.

2 Bring to a boil over high heat. Skim off any scum, then lower the heat to a gentle simmer. Cover and cook for 2½–3 hours.

3 Ladle the contents of the pot into a colander set over a large bowl. Allow the stock to strain through.

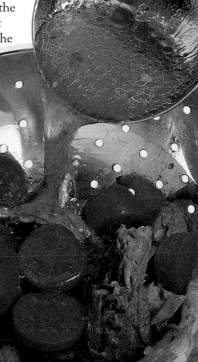

MEAT

One of the most important considerations when preparing meat is to make sure the cut and the cooking method are suitable for each other. This is the best way to guarantee good results.

ROASTS

PRIME CUTS ARE BEST for roasting, so reserve these for special occasions when economy is not a priority. For roasting temperatures and times of the joints shown here, plus other easy roasting joints, see page 160. For roasting and carving instructions, see pages 52–53.

Leg of lamb *sold whole or halved, on the bone. 3½–5½lb (1.5–2.5kg) whole leg serves 6–8; 2–3½lb (1–1.6kg) shank (knuckle) half or fillet end serves 4–6.*

Loin of pork *boned and rolled, with or without skin. If skin is scored, it will make crisp crackling. 4½–5½lb (2–2.5kg) roast serves 8–10; 2–3½lb (1–1.5kg) roast serves 4–6.*

Rib of beef *is a traditional cut for roast beef. A 2-rib, 5½lb (2.5kg) roast serves 4; a 10lb (4.5kg) roast with 3 ribs serves 8–10. Sirloin is another traditional roast.*

CUTS OF MEAT

MEAT THAT IS SOLD ALREADY CUT is both convenient and time-saving. Look for good butchering: steaks and chops should be well trimmed and similar in size so they cook in the same time. For each person allow ¼–½lb (125–250g) boneless meat, a little more if meat is on the bone.

Ground beef *(left) is suitable for burgers; medium-ground beef (right) is best for Bolognese sauce.*

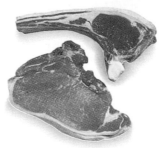

Chops *cook very quickly, and can be grilled or pan-fried. Lamb loin chops (top) have a succulent "eye" of meat; serve 2 per person. Pork loin chops (bottom) are larger; allow 1 per person.*

Steak *can be grilled, broiled, or pan-fried. Rump steak (right) is sold in large slices, which need to be cut. Fillet and sirloin are sold as individual steaks.*

Pork tenderloin, *also called fillet, can be cut into thin slices on the diagonal and pan-fried, or cut into thin strips and stir-fried.*

Braising steak *for casseroles and stews requires long, slow cooking. Stewing steak is more muscular, and needs longer cooking.*

Liver slices *can be pan-fried, stir-fried, or broiled. Calf's liver (left) is tender, but expensive; lamb's is cheaper.* **Lamb's kidneys** *(above) are for pan-frying and broiling on skewers; allow 2 per person.*

Preparing Meat

MEAT FROM THE BUTCHER or supermarket is usually sold trimmed and cut into serving portions or cubes, but there is often a little extra something you can do at home to make it look, cook, and taste better. Most meat is sold lean, but try to keep a thin layer or marbling of fat – no matter what the cooking method, this moistens the meat during cooking and improves flavor.

LAMB CHOPS

Slice off the excess fat with a chef's knife. Cut around the contours of the chop, leaving a thin layer of fat on the meat.

PORK CHOPS

Cut through the edging fat, making deep cuts with a chef's knife. The chops will fan out attractively while cooking.

RUMP STEAK

Cut edging fat at 1in (2cm) intervals with scissors. Snip through membrane under the fat to keep steak from curling.

BRAISING STEAK

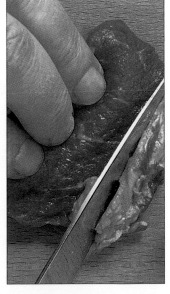

Trim off fat around edges of the meat with a chef's knife. This is easiest when the meat is still in one piece, before cubing.

Tender Cuts

TENDER, THIN MEAT is best for pan-fries and stir-fries that are cooked quickly over high heat. Pounding flattens the meat so it cooks quickly and is easy to slice; it also breaks down the fibers and helps tenderize the meat. Here a saucepan is used – the ideal shape for pounding without creating ridges. Rump steak is shown; pork tenderloin and boneless chicken breast can be prepared in the same way.

POUNDING

Place the meat between two sheets of waxed paper and pound with the bottom of a heavy saucepan.

SLICING

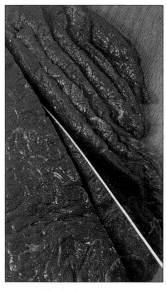

For stir-fries, pound the meat (see left), then slice across the grain into thin strips, about ¼in (5mm) wide.

Kidneys & Liver

RICH IN IRON AND PROTEIN, kidneys and liver require little in the way of preparation. Both need careful, fast cooking – a few minutes at the most. Kidneys and liver become tough if overcooked.

KIDNEYS

Peel fine membrane away and slice kidney lengthwise in half. Cut out piece of fat and tubes at core of kidney with a knife.

LIVER

Snip off any unsightly, ragged edges from slices of liver with scissors, then cut out any ducts with a paring knife.

MEAT

─ROASTING A LEG OF LAMB─

REMOVE THE MEAT from the refrigerator and let it stand, covered, at room temperature for about 30 minutes. If meat is taken straight from the refrigerator, it will be difficult to get an accurate result. For roasting temperatures and times, see page 160.

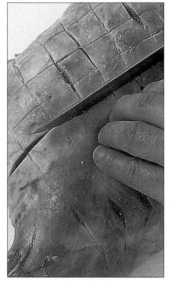 

1 Score a diamond pattern in the fat with a chef's knife. If you like, insert slivers of peeled garlic clove or sprigs of fresh rosemary into the cuts.

2 If you have a meat thermometer, push it into the thickest part of the lamb, away from the bone. Rub lamb with olive oil, salt, and pepper.

3 Roast on rack in a roasting pan. Halfway through, baste by spooning over the juices. At the end of roasting, insert knife into a thick part of the meat.

4 The juices that run out will be pink if the meat is medium-rare, clear if it is well-done. Check temperature if using a meat thermometer.

─CARVING A LEG OF LAMB─

MEAT SHOULD ALWAYS BE ALLOWED to stand after roasting and before carving. This gives time for the juices to settle, which makes the meat easy to carve; it also gives you time to make gravy with the cooking juices (see page 103). Use a carving fork and knife to slice the meat.

1 Lift the cooked lamb off the rack with two large spoons. Wrap it loosely in foil and let it stand in a warm place for about 15 minutes.

2 Place the lamb meat side up and cut a V-shaped wedge at the knuckle end. Cut slices away from this wedge, working toward the fillet end.

3 When all the slices are cut on the meaty side of the lamb, turn it over and cut horizontal slices, parallel to the bone.

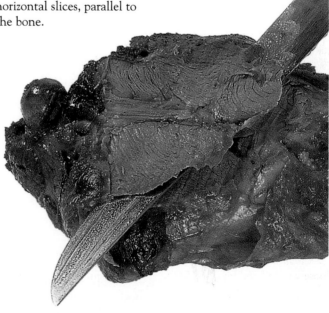

COOKING A BONED ROAST

BONED ROASTS ARE SOLD rolled and tied, which makes them easy to roast and carve. Good cuts for roasting are beef sirloin and tenderloin, and loin, leg, and shoulder cuts of both lamb and pork. Let the meat come to room temperature before preparing it for roasting. A meat thermometer can be used, but is not essential. Here, pork shoulder is rubbed with olive oil, pepper, and salt before roasting to make a spicy crust. For roasting temperatures and times, see page 160.

ROASTING A RIB OF BEEF

THIS IS AN EXCELLENT ROASTING CUT: the rib bones conduct heat so the meat cooks quickly without drying out. Let the meat come to room temperature before preparing it for roasting. Trim off all but a thin layer of fat, then rub with olive oil, salt, and crushed peppercorns. If you have a meat thermometer, insert in a thick part of the meat, away from the bones. Make the gravy (see page 103) while the meat is standing. For roasting temperatures and times, see page 160.

1 Rub the meat with a little olive oil, then with 4 tbsp crushed mixed peppercorns and 2 tbsp coarse sea salt.

2 Roast on a rack in a roasting pan, basting with the juices halfway. When done, snip strings with scissors.

1 Roast the beef in a roasting pan, with the ribs facing upward. Halfway through roasting, baste with the fat.

2 After roasting, juices will be pink if meat is rare, clear if medium or well-done. Wrap in foil; let stand for 15 minutes.

3 Pull off the strings and discard. Wrap the roast loosely in foil and let stand for 15 minutes while making the gravy (see page 103).

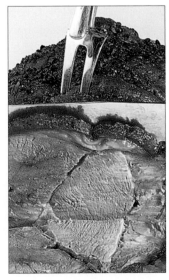

4 To carve, steady the joint by piercing it on the top with a carving fork. Carve neat slices with a carving knife, using a sawing action.

3 To carve, first free the meat from the bones. Start at the bone ends and work the knife between the meat and the bones, using a sawing action.

4 Once the meat is free of the bones, position it so that the fat is uppermost. Cut vertical slices with the knife, using a sawing action.

VEGETABLES

Buy small quantities of fresh vegetables frequently. Not only will

they taste better if they are as fresh as possible, they will also

be better for you: as vegetables age, their nutrients deteriorate.

— ONIONS —

THIS IS A SIMPLE TECHNIQUE used by chefs for chopping onions into uniform pieces. Unevenly chopped onions can adversely affect the look and texture of a dish.

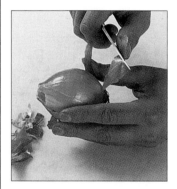

1 Cut off the top end, then peel off the papery outer skin with a paring knife until you reach the root end. Trim the root, but leave it in place.

2 Using a chef's knife, cut the onion lengthwise in half. Put one half, cut side down, on a board; hold it steady with one hand.

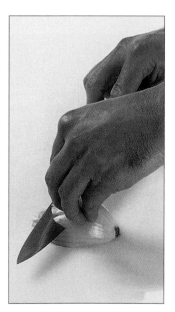

3 Make horizontal cuts through the onion, stopping short of the root. Make vertical cuts down the length of the onion, again avoiding the root.

4 Hold the onion firmly and slice it crosswise into dice. The thinner the slices, the finer the dice. If you like, use the root when making stock.

— GARLIC —

A HEAD OF GARLIC is made up of many cloves. Pry the cloves apart with your fingers before peeling and crushing them as shown. Purple-skinned garlic is best.

1 To peel a clove, lightly crush it with the flat side of a chef's knife to loosen the skin. Peel the skin from the clove with a paring knife.

2 Put the clove in a garlic press and squeeze the handles together. The flesh will be forced out through the holes in the grill.

— LEEKS —

SOIL IS OFTEN TRAPPED between the leaves of leeks, but it is rarely visible. If leek halves are required for a dish, the method shown here is the best way to clean them. If leeks are to be sliced, cut them in half, slice, then wash.

1 Cut off the tough top and root end; use in stock. The tops of small young leeks are more tender, and can be included with the white part.

2 Cut the leek lengthwise in half, then hold each half under cold running water and rinse thoroughly until there is no soil left between the leaves.

PEPPERS

SWEET PEPPERS COME IN MANY COLORS: red and green are the most common (red is a riper version of green) but yellow, orange, and even purple varieties are also available. All have a similar taste, but green peppers are the least sweet because they are the least ripe. Core peppers whole for stuffing and slicing into rings; halve before coring for slicing or chopping.

CORING WHOLE

Cut deep around the stem with a paring knife. Hold the stem and twist the core, using the knife to help pull out the core and seeds together. Discard.

HALVING & CORING

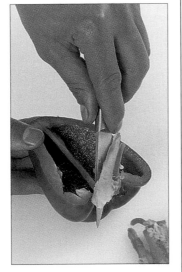

Cut the pepper lengthwise in half, then cut out the stem and core with a paring knife. Scrape away the white ribs and seeds from both halves.

TOMATOES

USE CANNED TOMATOES for cooking if you can't get juicy, ripe fresh tomatoes. Pale, wintertime tomatoes are often tasteless with thick skins and seeds that are difficult to remove. When a recipe calls for tomatoes to be peeled and seeded, first cut out the cores and score a cross in the base of each tomato, then use the method shown here.

1 Immerse the tomatoes in a pan of boiling water for 8–15 seconds, until the skins split. Transfer to a bowl of cold water with a slotted spoon.

2 Lift the tomatoes out one at a time. Pick up the edges of the skin with a knife, and peel off. To seed, halve the tomatoes and squeeze.

CHILIES

THE SMALLER THE CHILI, the hotter it will be. When handling chilies, avoid touching your eyes, and wash your hands, knife, and cutting board thoroughly afterward. For extra protection, wear rubber gloves.

1 Cut the chili lengthwise in half with a paring knife. Scrape out the seeds and membrane with the tip of the knife and discard.

2 Flatten the chili with your hand and slice lengthwise into strips. For diced chili, hold strips together and slice crosswise into equal-size cubes.

CELERY

A TIGHTLY FORMED HEAD OF CELERY with bright green leaves is the best choice. Fresh celery stalks snap easily: if they bend, they are past their best. Remove the tough outer strings from each stalk before using.

1 Trim off the leafy tops and separate the stalks by cutting off the root end. Discard any of the outer stalks that are damaged.

2 Working from the root end, make a shallow cut in each stalk with a serrated knife and pull down the tough outer strings to remove them.

VEGETABLES

AVOCADOS

FOR AVOCADO VINAIGRETTE and filled avocados, prepare as shown here. To use an avocado in a salad, halve and pit, then peel off the skin and slice or dice the flesh. For dips, halve and pit, then scoop out the flesh and mash it. Lemon juice helps prevent discoloration.

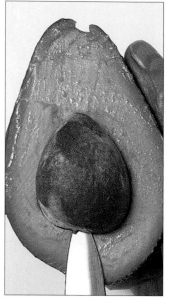

1 Using a chef's knife, cut lengthwise around the avocado through to the pit. Grip both halves and twist in opposite directions to separate.

2 Holding the half with the pit in one hand, embed the tip of a paring knife in the base of the pit and pry it out very carefully.

WINTER SQUASH

TWO OF THE BEST winter squash are acorn squash and pumpkin. Both have tough, inedible skin that is very difficult to cut, so remove it in sections as shown here with acorn squash. The firm flesh must be cooked thoroughly – either baked, boiled, or steamed.

1 Using a chef's knife, cut off the stem and bottom, then cut the squash crosswise in half. Scoop out seeds with a spoon. Cut each half into sections.

2 Using a paring knife, very carefully peel or carve off the skin from each section, then cut the flesh into pieces according to your recipe.

EGGPLANTS

SALTING EGGPLANTS before cooking draws out bitter juices and firms them so they absorb less oil, but is unnecessary in dishes with lots of vegetables and liquid, such as ratatouille. Eggplants may be pan-fried, broiled, or baked.

Peeling is unnecessary. Slice the eggplants crosswise into rounds ½in (1cm) thick. Discard the end pieces. Spread the slices out in a single layer in a large dish and sprinkle salt liberally over them. Let stand for about 30 minutes – drops of moisture will appear on the surface of the slices. Put the slices in a colander and rinse off the salty juices under cold running water. Pat the slices dry with paper towels before cooking.

ZUCCHINI

THESE SUMMER SQUASH have soft, edible skin and seeds. The tender flesh has a high water content and cooks quickly. Pan-frying, grilling, broiling, and baking are all suitable cooking methods.

Trim off both ends with a chef's knife. Small zucchini can be left whole or cut crosswise into rounds of uniform thickness. For large zucchini, cut lengthwise in half, then crosswise in half. If you like, cut these pieces into sticks. Large zucchini can also be cut lengthwise in half, hollowed out, and boiled for 2 minutes, then drained, stuffed, and baked in the oven.

MUSHROOMS

ALL MUSHROOMS deteriorate quickly, so use them as soon as possible, and prepare them just before cooking. They absorb water easily and can become soggy and waterlogged if washed, so wipe them rather than washing them. Most mushrooms sold in supermarkets are grown in sterile soil, so this method is safe. Peeling is unnecessary. To preserve flavor and texture, always cook mushrooms for the shortest possible time.

CULTIVATED

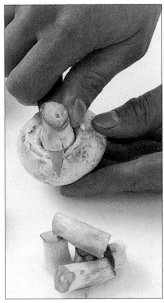 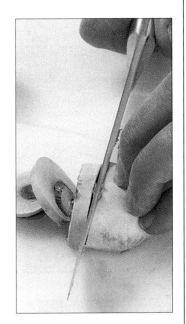

1 Wipe the mushrooms with a damp cloth to remove any soil. Trim off the stems with a paring knife.

2 Put each mushroom stem side down on a board. Cut downward into uniform slices with a chef's knife.

WILD

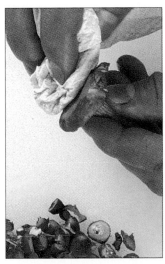 

1 Fresh wild mushrooms are delicate. Gently wipe with a damp cloth and trim off woody stem ends with a paring knife.

2 Cut mushrooms lengthwise in half with a chef's knife to preserve their attractive natural shape.

CARROTS & PARSNIPS

THESE ROOT VEGETABLES share a fibrous texture and a naturally sweet taste. First peel them with a vegetable peeler and trim off the ends with a chef's knife, then prepare as shown below. Carrot sticks and slices can be eaten raw; sticks are also good in stir-fries. Parsnips are always served cooked: boiled and mashed or parboiled and roasted like potatoes. For basic cooking instructions and times for carrots and parsnips, see page 161.

CARROTS

For sticks, cut lengthwise into thin slices with a chef's knife, then stack the slices and cut lengthwise into sticks.

For slices, cut crosswise into rounds with a chef's knife. For quick, even cooking, make the rounds about ¼in (5mm) thick.

PARSNIPS

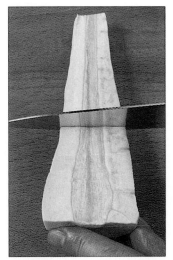 

1 Using a chef's knife, cut in half lengthwise, then crosswise. Each parsnip yields two wide and two thin pieces.

2 For old parsnips, stand each piece upright and cut in half, then cut away the triangle of woody core.

VEGETABLES

——— CABBAGE & BROCCOLI ———

BRUSSELS SPROUTS are a kind of cabbage. Together with broccoli, they belong to the brassica family and are a good source of nutrients. Eat them raw or lightly cooked. For basic cooking instructions and times, see page 161.

LEAFY CABBAGE

Cut lengthwise into quarters and remove core from the base of each piece. Separate the leaves and remove the thick central rib from each.

HEAD CABBAGE

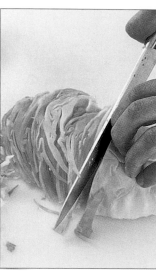

Cut lengthwise into quarters with a chef's knife, then remove the core at the base of each piece. Cut the quarters crosswise into strips.

BROCCOLI

Break the florets off the central stalk with your hands. Cut into 2–3 smaller florets with a paring knife, then cut off the stalks and thinly slice them.

BRUSSELS SPROUTS

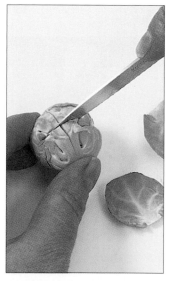

Trim the bottoms. Remove any discolored outer leaves and discard. To cook large sprouts evenly, cut a cross in the base with a paring knife.

——— SPINACH ———

SPINACH WEIGHS VERY LITTLE and looks like a large amount when raw, but it shrinks a lot during cooking. For four people, 1¼lb (600g) is usual. Young, tender leaves can be eaten raw in salads; allow ½lb (200g) for four.

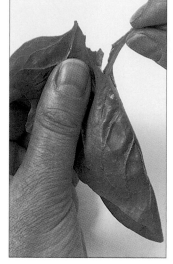

1 To remove the central ribs, fold each leaf lengthwise along the rib with the rib facing outward. Tear the rib away from the leaf and discard.

2 Rinse the leaves under cold water, then place in a large pot with only the water that clings to the leaves. Push down tightly and sprinkle with salt.

3 Cover with a tight-fitting lid and cook over medium heat for 3–5 minutes, or until tender. Hold the lid and shake the pot often during cooking.

4 Tip contents of pot into a colander. Press hard with a spatula to remove as much water as possible. Return to the pot and toss until hot and dry.

GREEN BEANS

GREEN BEANS ARE EATEN WHOLE or sliced. Scarlet runners are cut on the diagonal. Fava beans are removed from the pod first, and the pod is discarded before cooking. All fresh green beans should snap easily when bent in half; if not, they have been stored too long or picked old. Boiling is the usual cooking method for all green beans, for the briefest possible cooking time. For basic cooking instructions and times, see page 161.

FAVA BEANS

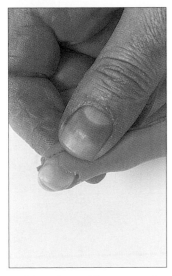

Holding the pod between index finger and thumb, push beans out until the end of the pod is reached. If the beans have visible skin, peel it off.

SCARLET RUNNERS

Trim the beans, then cut off the strings from the side with a serrated knife. Slice the beans on the diagonal with a paring knife.

FRENCH BEANS

1 Using your fingers, gently break off the ends of each bean. Leave the beans whole, or cut them into short pieces (see right).

2 To cut French beans, line up several beans together in a tight bunch. With a chef's knife, slice diagonally across into equal-size pieces.

PEAS

FRESH PEAS ARE MOST TENDER YOUNG, when they are sweet and crunchy. Snow peas (also called mangetouts) and sugar snaps are cultivated to be harvested before the peas are fully developed, so they are meant to be eaten whole with the pod. Some very young ones have no strings and need no preparation at all – these are excellent for stir-frying, whole or sliced. For basic cooking instructions and times, see page 161.

SNOW PEAS & SUGAR SNAPS

1 Break off the stem with your fingers and gently pull down one side to remove the string. Leave whole, or slice on the diagonal (see right).

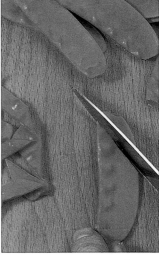

2 To slice, cut diagonally across into equal-size pieces with a chef's knife. For stir-fries, diamond-shape pieces look most attractive.

SHELLING PEAS

When removing fresh peas from the pod, work over a large bowl. Press the base of the pod to open, then run your thumb under the peas until they are released.

VEGETABLES

PEELING POTATOES

LARGE, MATURE POTATOES are usually peeled before cooking if they are to be mashed or roasted. New potatoes should be scrubbed. For safety information, see page 162.

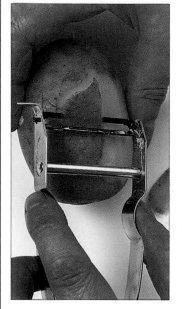 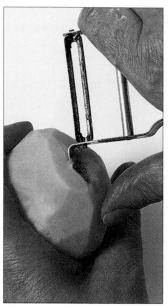

1 Hold the potato firmly. Using a vegetable peeler, drag the blade over the potato in short, sharp strokes to remove a thin layer of skin.

2 Use the triangular piece of metal on the side of the peeler to dig out any indented pieces of skin left by the peeler; these are called "eyes."

BOILING POTATOES

USE JUST ENOUGH WATER to cover the potatoes. Start timing when the water boils after adding the potatoes. Allow 2lb (1kg) potatoes and 1 tsp salt for 4–6 people.

1 For even cooking, cut the potatoes into even-size chunks. Put old potatoes in salted cold water, new potatoes in salted boiling water.

2 Cover and simmer gently for 15–20 minutes, or until the potatoes feel tender when pierced with the tip of a paring knife. Drain immediately.

MASHED POTATOES

THE BEST POTATOES for mashing are mature, floury kinds. For 4–6 people, use 2lb (1kg) potatoes, 1 tsp salt, scant 1 cup (200ml) hot milk, and 3–4 tbsp butter.

1 Peel, boil, and drain the potatoes (see left); return the potatoes to the pot. Heat the milk in a small pan until hot, then pour over potatoes.

2 Add the butter or, if you prefer, 2–3 tbsp olive oil. Mash vigorously with a potato masher, or use a handheld electric mixer.

3 Continue working until all the lumps have gone and the potatoes are smooth.

MAKING FRENCH FRIES

THE SAFEST WAY TO COOK FRENCH FRIES is in an electric deep-fat fryer with a thermostatic control. Always read the manufacturer's instructions carefully. The secret is to fry them first at a low temperature to cook the potatoes through, then again at a higher temperature to crisp the outside. Use mature, floury varieties of potato for making fries. For four people, use 1½lb (750g) potatoes.

1 Cut the potatoes into slices ¼in (5mm) thick, then into sticks ¼in (5mm) wide. Soak in cold water for 10 minutes, then drain and dry well.

2 Heat oil to 325°F (160°C). Put the potatoes in the fryer basket and lower it into the oil. Cook for 5 minutes, until soft. Lift out and test with a knife.

3 Heat the oil to 375°F (190°C). Lower the basket back into the oil. Deep-fry for 3–4 minutes, until crisp and brown. Drain on paper towels.

ROASTING POTATOES

MATURE, FLOURY POTATOES are best for roasting. Use 2lb (1kg) for 4–6 people. Preheat the oven to 425°F (220°C). Peel the potatoes and cut them into even-size pieces. Place in a pot of salted cold water, bring to a boil, then drain – this is called parboiling. Put 3 tbsp sunflower oil in a roasting pan and put in the preheated oven for about 5 minutes, until very hot.

1 Lift the pan out of the oven, add the potatoes, and turn with a spoon and fork to coat in the hot oil. Return the pan to the oven for 5–10 minutes.

2 Shake the pan gently (to keep the potatoes from sticking). Roast for 45 minutes until crisp, turning occasionally. Lift out with a slotted spoon.

BAKING POTATOES

LARGE, FLOURY POTATOES are good for baking in their skins because they have a light, fluffy texture. When cooked, split and add butter or a filling of your choice.

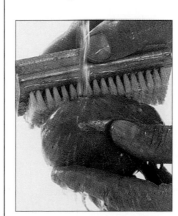 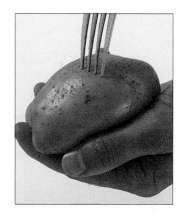

1 Preheat oven to 425°F (220°C). Scrub potatoes under cold running water. Remove any "eyes" (see Peeling on facing page).

2 Prick each potato several times to prevent bursting. Bake for 1–1¼ hours, until soft all the way through. Test by squeezing with your hands.

FRUIT

A wide variety of fresh fruit is now available in supermarkets all
year. High in fiber and vitamins, fruit is essential to a
healthy diet. Eat fruit raw or cooked in sweet and savory dishes.

— APPLES & PEARS —

TO HELP PREVENT discoloration after peeling or cutting
apples and pears, brush exposed surfaces with citrus
juice – lemon, lime, or orange. Apples and pears quickly
turn brown on exposure to air.

CORING APPLES WHOLE

1 Hold the fruit steady with
one hand and center the
corer over the apple stem.
Push corer firmly down into
the base of the apple.

2 Pull the corer up, twisting
firmly to remove the core
and seeds. Stuff the center of
the apple immediately, before
it begins to turn brown.

CORING PEAR HALVES

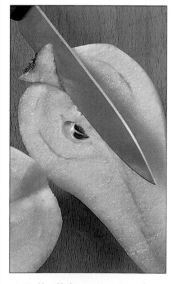

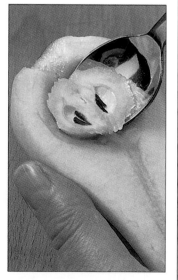

1 Pull off the stem. Cut the
pear lengthwise in half.
Make two diagonal cuts on
each side of the base and
remove this from both halves.

2 Scoop out the core and
seeds using a teaspoon.
Run the handle of the spoon
along the center of each pear
half to remove stringy fibers.

— SLICING APPLES —

IF YOU NEED SLICED APPLES for a pie or crepe filling or a
fruit salad, the technique shown here is the quickest
and easiest way to prepare them. It works well for both
dessert and cooking apples.

1 Use a paring knife to cut the
apples lengthwise in half and
again into quarters. Make a
diagonal cut to the center on
each side; remove the cores.

2 Working quickly to
prevent the apples from
discoloring, peel each apple
quarter with a paring knife
or vegetable peeler.

3 Cut each apple quarter
lengthwise into even,
crescent-shape slices. Cut
toward you, following the
shape of the crescent.

4 Peeled apple slices will
discolor quickly. Toss them
in lemon juice to help keep
them moist and prevent them
from turning brown.

PITTING FRUIT

PLUMS, PEACHES, NECTARINES, and apricots usually need their pits removed when used in a recipe. The flesh often clings to the pit, especially if the fruit is not very ripe: the technique shown here helps overcome this. Always brush fruit with citrus juice once it has been cut, to help prevent discoloration. The mango has a large, flat pit that is slightly off-center. It requires a special technique to remove it.

REMOVING THE PIT

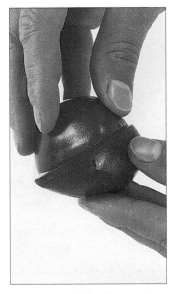 

1 Cut around the fruit with a paring knife, following the indentation; cut down to the pit. Hold the fruit and twist each half in opposite directions.

2 Loosen the pit by prying it up with the tip of the knife, then lift it out with your fingers. Thin skin can be left on or peeled off.

PREPARING MANGOES

1 Use a chef's knife to cut the fruit vertically along one side of the flat pit. Repeat on the opposite side to make three pieces of mango.

2 Cut away the flesh from all sides of the piece with the pit in. Remove the skin from all pieces with a paring knife, then slice or chop the flesh.

BERRIES & CURRANTS

PUSH CURRANTS off their stems with a fork, then rinse and dry them as shown below for strawberries. All berries can be prepared in this way except raspberries, which have very delicate, soft flesh and should not be rinsed because rinsing takes away their flavor. Do not prepare berries and currants more than 2 hours before use. Once prepared, store them in a covered container in the refrigerator because they deteriorate very quickly.

STRAWBERRIES

1 Pull out the green hull from the top of each fruit, using the tip of a paring knife to help if the hull is difficult to remove. Discard the hull.

2 Rinse in a colander under cold running water as briefly as possible. Shake the colander gently so the fruit is not bruised.

3 Line a tray with a double thickness of paper towels. Spread the fruit out on the paper and shake the tray gently so the fruit dries on all sides.

FRUIT

—PREPARING CITRUS FRUIT—

SHINY, PLUMP FRUIT with firm, blemish-free skin are best for zest. Thin-skinned fruit will yield the most juice. Buy unwaxed fruit for zesting if possible, or scrub fruit with a brush under cold water and dry well.

ZEST

To use a zester, pull zester toward you, applying pressure firmly. To avoid pith, do not press too deeply into the rind.

To use a box grater, rub the fruit gently over the small cutters. Remove the rind from the grater with a pastry brush.

SQUEEZING JUICE

1 Firmly press halved fruit over a lemon squeezer and twist until all the juice is extracted. If the fruit is warm it will yield more juice.

2 Remove the strainer and discard the seeds and pith. If not using immediately, store the juice in a covered container in the refrigerator.

—SEGMENTING CITRUS FRUIT—

TO REMOVE ALL THE BITTER WHITE PITH AND MEMBRANE from an orange, this method of segmenting is favored by chefs. Always work over a bowl to catch the juice. For round slices, cut crosswise after peeling in step 1.

ORANGE

1 Cut peel from both ends of the fruit with a chef's knife. Stand fruit upright; cut away peel following contour of fruit.

2 Working over a bowl, cut down both sides of each membrane with a paring knife to free segments from the core.

GRAPEFRUIT

1 Cut the fruit crosswise in half. Using a small serrated knife, cut down between the flesh and the inner pith. Work the knife all round the fruit.

2 Starting with the tip of the knife in the center, cut down both sides of each membrane. This will free the segments for easy eating.

PINEAPPLE

REMOVING PINEAPPLE SKIN requires a sharp chef's knife. The skin is hard and tough, so be careful to grip the knife firmly and to cut with a slow sawing motion. Lay the pineapple down on a chopping board and slice off the top and bottom first so the fruit will stand upright before attempting to cut off the skin. An alternative method for preparing a pineapple is to cut it into crosswise slices after step 1. Lay each slice flat and stamp out the core with a small cutter.

MELON

ALWAYS CHILL MELONS in a plastic bag in the refrigerator before cutting. If not wrapped, they will taint other foods. Cut melons into wedges as shown here and serve them as they are for a first course, or use the slices in fruit salads. Alternatively, peel wedges of melon and cut lengthwise into even slices, then fan them out on a plate. Small melons can be simply cut in half and seeded as in step 1, then served as they are for a first course, or filled with fruit for a dessert.

1 Stand the fruit upright and cut off the skin. Follow the contours of the fruit, removing as many of the spikes and as little of the flesh as possible.

2 Cut the pineapple in half lengthwise, then lay each half flat side down on the board and cut lengthwise in half again to make quarters.

1 Hold fruit steady with one hand and cut lengthwise in half with a chef's knife. Use a large spoon to remove membrane and seeds.

2 Scrape the center of the melon halves completely clean with the spoon, then cut lengthwise in half again to make quarters.

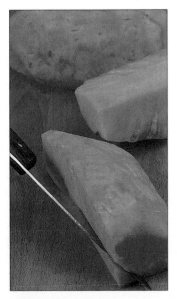

3 Cut away the fibrous core from the center of each quarter. On young fruit, cores are tender enough to be eaten; otherwise discard them.

4 Slice each quarter crosswise into chunks of preferred thickness. If you like, cut these slices in half to make smaller pieces.

3 Make a cut between the inner edge of the rind and the flesh at one end. Continue cutting to the other end, using a sawing action with the knife.

4 Slice detached melon flesh into pieces of equal thickness. If you like, cut these slices in half to make smaller pieces.

65

SHORTCRUST PASTRY

Making your own pastry is a satisfying task. Once you have

mastered the technique, you will be able to create

an impressive range of quiches, tarts, and double-crust pies.

CUTTING IN FAT

HAVE YOUR KITCHEN, ingredients, and utensils cool, and handle the pastry as little as possible. The quantity here is enough for one 9in (23cm) double-crust pie. Use half this amount for an 8in (20cm) pastry case (see facing page). Pastry can also be made well in a food processor.

ADDING WATER

USE COLD WATER and add it gradually because you may not need it all. If the dough is too dry it will crack, if too much water is added it will be sticky – in both cases it will be difficult to roll out. Work quickly and lightly, using a round-bladed dinner knife for mixing.

1 Place 2¾ cups (350g) all-purpose flour in a bowl. Cut ¾ cup (175g) hard margarine into cubes; add it to the flour.

2 Using your fingertips, rub the fat and flour together, reaching to the bottom of bowl to incorporate all the flour.

1 Add about 6 tbsp (90ml) cold water, 1 tbsp at a time. Mix each one in with a knife before adding the next.

2 Enough water has been added when the mixture just begins to hold together in a soft mass.

3 Continue cutting in, occasionally shaking the bowl to bring any large pieces of fat to the surface.

4 When all the fat has been cut in, the mixture will look like bread crumbs. Now add the water (see right).

3 Using the fingertips of one hand, gently gather the mixture together against the side of the bowl.

4 Put the pastry onto the work surface and very gently shape and pat it into a rough ball.

MAKING A PASTRY SHELL

HALF THE AMOUNT OF PASTRY made on the facing page is a generous quantity to make a pastry shell in an 8in (20cm) loose-bottomed quiche pan. Be careful not to stretch the pastry when rolling it out or lining the pan, or the pastry will shrink as it cooks. After you have lined the pan, chill the pastry shell in the refrigerator for about 30 minutes, or freeze it for about 15 minutes. This sets the shape before baking and so helps prevent shrinkage.

BAKING PASTRY EMPTY

FOR A CRISP BASE to quiches and tarts, the pastry shell is often baked without its filling. Lining the case with aluminum foil and filling it with baking beans keeps the pastry shell from rising up. This technique is called "baking empty" or "baking blind." The baking beans can be either the ceramic commercially made variety or dried beans or peas from your pantry. Whichever kind you choose, they can be used over and over again.

1 Push the loose base out of the pan. Dredge the ring and base with flour. Put the pastry in the middle of the base.

2 Flatten and roll out the pastry so it overhangs the base by 2in (5cm) all around. Fold in the overhanging pastry.

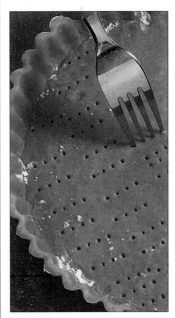

1 Prick the pastry all over the base with a fork. Cut a large square of foil and line the pastry shell with it.

2 Fill the foil lining with baking beans and spread them out evenly. Bake at 425°F (220°C) for about 10 minutes.

3 Replace the base in the pan with the pastry on it. Fold the extra pastry back over the edge of the pan.

4 Roll the rolling pin over the top of the pan, pressing down firmly. The edges of the pan will trim the pastry neatly.

3 The pastry edges should be a pale cookie color; if not, bake for a few minutes more. Lift out the foil and beans.

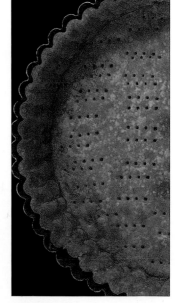

4 Bake the empty shell for 10 minutes more, or until the base is a pale cookie color. Cool in the pan.

SAUCES

Homemade sauces taste better than any you can buy. These basic
sauces are easy to master and invaluable for serving as an
accompaniment or for using in recipes. For gravy, see page 103.

WHITE SAUCE

THE CONSISTENCY OF THIS SAUCE is medium-thick. Use
2 tbsp each butter and flour for a thin sauce, or 4 tbsp for
a thick sauce. Makes about 2½ cups (600ml).

INGREDIENTS

3 tbsp butter

⅓ cup (40g) all-purpose flour

2½ cups (600ml) hot milk

seasoning

1 Melt the butter in a
saucepan over medium
heat until foaming. Sprinkle
in the flour.

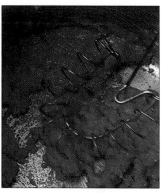

2 Using a coil whisk,
whisk the mixture (called a
roux) for 1–2 minutes. Remove
the pan from the heat.

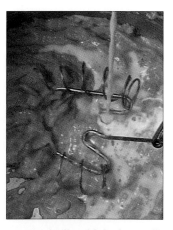

3 Gradually add the hot milk,
whisking constantly. Return
to medium heat and whisk
until boiling and thickened.

4 Check that sauce is
smooth. Season according
to your recipe with salt, pepper,
mustard, or nutmeg.

CUSTARD

THIS IS THE WAY to make smooth, creamy custard, using
eggs and a vanilla bean. Makes about 2 cups (500ml).

INGREDIENTS

1¾ cups (400ml) milk

1 vanilla bean, split lengthwise

3 large egg yolks

¼ cup (50g) superfine sugar

2 tsp cornstarch

1 Heat the milk over medium
heat until hot. Turn off the
heat and add the vanilla bean.
Cover and infuse 20 minutes.

2 Beat the egg yolks, sugar,
and cornstarch with a
balloon whisk until combined.
Remove the vanilla bean.

3 Whisk the milk into the
egg yolk mixture. Return
to the pan and stir over low
heat with a wooden spoon.

4 Cook for about 5 minutes,
stirring constantly, until
the custard is smooth and
coats the back of the spoon.

MAYONNAISE

THE METHOD BELOW is for making mayonnaise in a food processor, but if you don't have a machine, it can be made by hand. If you make it by hand, use an egg yolk only rather than a whole egg, and make sure all the ingredients are at room temperature. Put the yolk in a bowl with the mustard, wine vinegar, and seasoning and add the oil a drop at a time, whisking continuously with a balloon whisk until the mixture begins to thicken. Continue whisking in the oil in a steady stream until the mayonnaise is thick and smooth. Whisk in the lemon juice. For safety information on raw eggs, see page 162.

INGREDIENTS

1 large egg
1 tsp Dijon mustard
1 tbsp white wine vinegar
salt and pepper
1¼ cups (325ml) sunflower oil
juice of ½ lemon

1 Put the egg, mustard, vinegar, and seasoning in a processor with the metal blade; process until blended.

2 With the machine on full speed, gradually add the oil through the feed tube in a steady stream.

3 When the mayonnaise is thick, remove the lid, add the lemon juice, and process to combine. Check seasoning. Store in a covered container in the refrigerator for up to 3 days.

FRENCH DRESSING

THIS DRESSING, called *vinaigrette* in French, is a classic salad dressing and is very quick and easy to make. It will keep in the refrigerator for up to 1 month, so it is worth making a large batch. Store it in a screw-top jar and shake to re-mix before using. For really good flavor, use the best extra-virgin olive oil and a good wine vinegar, and if you prefer extra texture you can use a coarse-grain mustard instead of smooth Dijon. The nicest leafy herbs to use are tarragon, basil, and parsley. The quantity of dressing made here is enough for two large green or mixed salads each serving four to six people.

INGREDIENTS

2 tbsp wine vinegar
2 tsp Dijon mustard
1–2 tsp superfine sugar
salt and pepper
6 tbsp (90ml) extra-virgin olive oil
1 tbsp chopped leafy fresh herbs

1 Place the vinegar, mustard, 1 tsp sugar, and salt and pepper in a bowl. Combine by whisking with a coil whisk.

2 Continue whisking the mixture vigorously until the ingredients are evenly combined and thick.

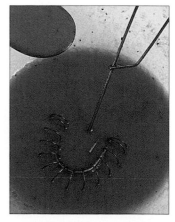

3 Add the olive oil slowly in a thin, steady stream, whisking vigorously until it is all incorporated.

4 Taste the dressing, and add more sugar and salt and pepper if you like. Stir in the herbs just before serving.

CRUMBS & CROUTONS

Leftover bread should never go to waste – it can be used to make

bread crumbs for coating delicate foods, stuffings for poultry and

meat, and croutons to garnish salads and soups.

BREAD CRUMBS

FINE CRUMBS FOR COATINGS and stuffings are best made in a food processor. Use day-old bread because fresh bread will stick in a ball. Use a box grater to make coarser crumbs, or push the bread through a sieve.

1 For coating food, pure white bread crumbs look best, so cut off crusts first. For stuffings, crusts can be left on: they give color and texture.

2 Tear 3 slices of bread into a food processor fitted with the metal blade. Process until fine. This will make about ¼ cup (75g) bread crumbs.

DRIED BREAD CRUMBS

WHEN BREAD CRUMBS ARE DRIED, they give a crisper coating than fresh crumbs, and this takes only a little extra time. If you prefer, dry slices of bread in the oven first, then process into crumbs – the result is the same.

1 Process day-old bread into fine crumbs (see above), then tip them onto a baking sheet. Spread them out in an even layer with your hands.

2 Bake at 300°F (150°C) for about 20 minutes, or until golden, shaking sheet once or twice to ensure that crumbs brown evenly.

CROUTONS

YOU CAN BUY commercially made croutons, but the homemade ones are both easy and economical, and they taste better. The technique shown here is a clever way to make croutons using a very small quantity of oil.

1 Stack 2 slices of day-old bread and cut off the crusts. Cut bread lengthwise, then crosswise into cubes.

2 Place the bread cubes in a plastic bag with 1–2 tbsp sunflower oil. Seal the bag and shake it vigorously.

3 Toss croutons in a nonstick sauté pan over medium heat until golden.

LEAVES & HERBS

All green salad leaves and herbs are delicate and can easily

be bruised, so always prepare them with care, and

store in the refrigerator to keep them garden fresh.

LETTUCE

TO AVOID BRUISING delicate leaves, they should be torn, not cut with a knife, and the larger the pieces, the less chance there is of bruising. To keep lettuce crisp, store it in a plastic bag in the refrigerator for up to 12 hours.

1 Use a small serrated knife to cut around the circular core at the base of the lettuce. Remove the core with the tip of the knife and discard.

2 Insert your thumbs into the hole left by the core and gently pull the lettuce apart into two halves. Separate the leaves from one another.

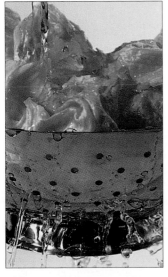

3 Place the leaves in a colander and rinse them under cold running water. Shake the colander and gently move the leaves around.

4 Dry the leaves by shaking them in the colander until there is no visible water, then gently tear them into pieces with your fingers.

FRESH HERBS

DELICATE, LEAFY FRESH HERBS are best prepared just before use, to keep them from drying out or discoloring. Add them to cooked dishes just before serving as they lose their flavor if cooked for any length of time.

CHOPPING

For robust herbs, strip the leaves from the stalks. Hold the tip of the chef's knife and chop the leaves by rocking the blade up and down against the board.

SNIPPING

For chives, which have hollow stems, use kitchen scissors to cut. Hold a small bunch over a bowl and finely snip them into the bowl.

SHREDDING BASIL

For soft-leaved basil, prevent bruising by gently rolling leaves together in a cigar shape, then cutting crosswise into strips with a paring knife.

BOUQUET GARNI

To make a bouquet garni, hold together 2–3 sprigs of thyme, 1 bay leaf, and 5–6 parsley stalks. Wind a piece of string around herbs and tie securely.

IN THIS CHAPTER you will find twelve Master Recipes, a collection designed to provide you with a range of cooking skills and meals to suit every occasion. Equipped with these, you will be able to make a simple supper just for yourself or a full-scale lunch or party dish for family and friends. Each recipe starts with detailed information on preparation, ingredients, and cooking techniques, plus a close-up photograph of the finished dish, then follows with photographs and captions that guide you through the directions every step of the way. Be methodical and follow the recipe carefully. When you have a little more experience, try the variations suggested, or experiment with your own creative combinations.

MASTER RECIPES

MASTER RECIPE

CLASSIC FRENCH OMELET

Nothing could be simpler or quicker to prepare than an omelet; with just a few basic ingredients you can whip up a delicious impromptu meal. The classic French omelet is plain, but the possibilities for flavorings and fillings are endless. Here, the French combination of herbs, known as *fines herbes*, is added.

COOK'S NOTES

Preparation time
3 minutes

Cooking time
No more than 1¼–1½ minutes

Special equipment
Nonstick omelet pan
with curved sides

Nutritional information
Calories: 281
Total fat: 23g of which
unsaturated fat: 10g
saturated fat: 10g
Sodium: 327mg

Taste tips
Fines herbes is a mixture of herbs
consisting of equal quantities of
chives, chervil, parsley, and
tarragon. The chives should be
snipped and the rest of the herbs
finely chopped.

KEYS TO SUCCESS

■ Use the right size pan. To serve one, use 2 large eggs in a 6¼in (16cm) omelet pan, or 3 eggs in the same pan for a more substantial meal. Too large a pan gives a thin, dry omelet. Too small, and the omelet will be leathery underneath and uncooked on top.

■ Combine the eggs by gentle stirring: do not overbeat. Vigorous beating adds air to the mixture and makes the omelet rubbery.

■ Preheat the pan over high heat until very hot so that the omelet will cook fast, in the French style.

■ An omelet is at its best when freshly made. Once it is out of the pan, it quickly gets cold and the texture becomes rubbery. Each one should be served and eaten right after cooking.

INGREDIENTS

SERVES 1

2 large eggs

1 tbsp chopped fresh herbs

1 tbsp water

salt and pepper

pat of butter

OMELETTE AUX FINES HERBES is a classic French omelet with herbs, served here with a leafy salad.

TECHNIQUES

Cracking eggs: page 34
Chopping and snipping
herbs: page 71

CLASSIC FRENCH OMELET

1 CRACK THE EGGS into a bowl, then add the chopped fresh herbs, water, and salt and pepper. Stir gently with a fork, just enough to break up the yolks and whites.

2 HEAT AN OMELET PAN over high heat for about 30 seconds, or until very hot. Add the butter; it will quickly start to foam. Tilt the pan so the butter coats the bottom.

5 CONTINUE FOR ABOUT 1–1¼ minutes until the omelet holds together and there is not enough liquid to flow into the spaces. At this stage it will still be runny on top.

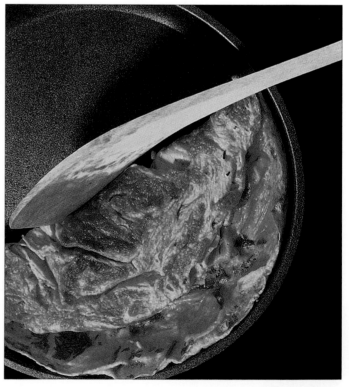

6 TILT THE OMELET PAN to one side and use the spatula to fold about one third of the omelet over. Jiggle the pan gently so that the omelet slides to the edge.

3 As soon as the butter has melted and stopped foaming – the sizzling sound will subside – pour in the egg and herb mixture. Tilt the pan to spread egg over the bottom.

4 After about 10 seconds, use a wooden spatula to begin to pull the cooked egg from the edge toward the center, allowing the liquid egg to flow into the space.

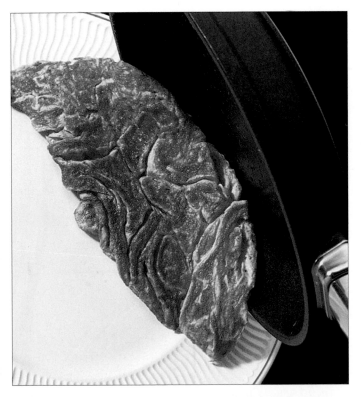

7 Bring a plate up to the pan. Tip the pan more so the omelet rolls over and falls onto the plate. The two edges should end up tucked neatly underneath.

VARIATIONS

Cheddar Cheese
Omit the herbs.
Sprinkle the omelet with ¼ cup (30g) grated Cheddar cheese at the end of step 5.

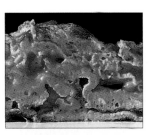

Watercress & Blue Cheese
Omit the herbs.
Sprinkle 4 tbsp chopped watercress and ¼ cup (30g) grated blue cheese onto the omelet at the end of step 5.

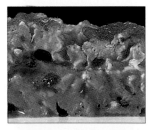

Ham & Gruyère
Omit the herbs.
Sprinkle the omelet with 2oz (50g) cooked ham, chopped into small pieces, and ¼ cup (30g) grated Gruyère cheese at the end of step 5.

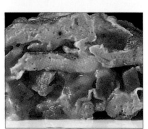

LEEK & POTATO SOUP

A good homemade soup tastes so much better than a canned one, and this one is quick and easy to make. It freezes well, too, so it is a good idea to make more than you need. Serve with chunks of crusty bread for lunch or supper, or swirl in a little extra cream for an elegant first course.

COOK'S NOTES

Prepare ahead
The soup can be made and kept, covered, in the refrigerator for up to 3 days, or frozen for up to 3 months

Preparation time
10–15 minutes to prepare the vegetables

Cooking time
30 minutes to cook the soup and reheat after puréeing

Special equipment
Large pot
Electric handheld blender

Nutritional information
Calories: 293
Total fat: 13g of which
unsaturated fat: 4g
saturated fat: 8g
Sodium: 349mg

Serving tips
When leek and potato soup is served chilled, it is known as vichyssoise. For a velvety, smooth finish, press the soup through a sieve after puréeing, let cool, then cover and chill in the refrigerator for at least 4 hours. Chilling dulls the flavor, so taste the soup before serving and add salt, pepper, nutmeg, or cream as necessary. Snipped chives are the classic garnish for vichyssoise.

TECHNIQUES

Leeks: page 54
Onions: page 54
Peeling potatoes: page 60
Chicken stock: page 49
Squeezing lemon juice: page 64
Chopping herbs: page 71

KEYS TO SUCCESS

■ Use homemade stock if you can; it gives depth of flavor. If this is not available, use 2 bouillon cubes dissolved in 5 cups (1.2 liters) boiling water. Canned chicken broth is a good alternative, but more expensive. Vegetable stock can be used instead of chicken, and gives a lighter taste.

■ To achieve a really smooth and creamy result, make sure that all the ingredients are soft before you purée the soup. Any pieces of undercooked vegetable will give the finished soup a lumpy texture.

■ When using a handheld blender, make the soup in the largest pot you have and keep the blades under the level of the soup while puréeing. This will help keep splashes to a minimum.

■ If you do not have an electric handheld blender, use a food processor or a freestanding blender, but cool the soup slightly first and purée it in batches. If you have none of these, place a sieve over a large bowl. Pour the soup in and press the solids through with the back of a spoon.

INGREDIENTS

3 leeks (about ½lb / 250g)

1 medium onion

2 tbsp butter

1lb (500g) potatoes

5 cups (1.2 liters) chicken stock

salt and pepper

nutmeg

½ cup (150ml) light cream

1 tsp lemon juice

2 tbsp chopped fresh parsley, to garnish

A BOWL OF GOOD HOMEMADE
SOUP *will be equally welcome for a
simple lunch or supper, or
for sophisticated entertaining.*

LEEK & POTATO SOUP

1 TRIM THE LEEKS, leaving some green at the top to color the soup. Cut in half lengthwise, then cut across into ¼ in (5mm) slices. Rinse in a colander in plenty of cold running water.

2 PEEL THE ONION and cut into slices about the same thickness as the leeks. Melt the butter in a large saucepan over medium heat until foaming, then add the leeks and onion.

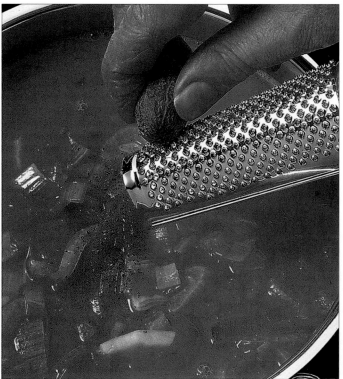

5 AS SOON AS you have added the potatoes, pour in the stock, then add salt and pepper. Do not use too much salt because the stock may already contain some.

6 ADD AROUND 8 gratings of nutmeg, turn up the heat, and bring to a boil. Reduce the heat, cover the pan, and simmer for about 10 minutes, or until the vegetables are soft.

3 STIR TO COAT the vegetables in butter. Cover the pan and cook over medium heat for about 10 minutes, or until soft but not brown, lifting the lid occasionally to stir.

4 WHILE THE LEEKS and onion are cooking, peel the potatoes and cut them into ¼ in (5mm) slices. When the leeks and onion are ready, add the potato slices to the pan.

7 REMOVE THE PAN from the heat. Using an electric handheld blender, with the blades held below the level of the soup, purée the soup for about 3 minutes, until smooth.

8 RETURN THE SOUP to medium heat and stir until it boils. Take off the heat, add the cream and lemon juice, then stir and check seasoning. Serve hot, sprinkled with parsley.

TAGLIATELLE BOLOGNESE

Named after the city of Bologna in northern Italy, Bolognese

is a rich, meaty sauce based on beef and *soffritto* – a finely

chopped mixture of celery, onion, carrot, and garlic.

Here it is served in the traditional way with tagliatelle,

but it can be served with other pasta such as spaghetti or penne.

COOK'S NOTES

Prepare ahead
The sauce can be made and kept, covered, in the refrigerator for up to 3 days, or frozen for up to 3 months

Preparation time
10 minutes to prepare the vegetables

Cooking time
About 1¼ hours

Special equipment
Large pot or casserole for making sauce
Large pot for boiling pasta
Spaghetti tongs: these are useful for serving long pasta shapes, but not essential

Nutritional information
Calories: 567
Total fat: 29g of which
unsaturated fat: 16g
saturated fat: 10g
Sodium: 173mg

Shopping tips
Fresh Parmesan cheese is expensive, but infinitely superior to the cheaper pre-grated varieties. Buy it in chunks and either grate it with a box grater (fine or coarse as you wish) or shave off curls with a vegetable peeler as and when needed.

TECHNIQUES

Celery: page 55
Onions: page 54
Carrots: page 57
Garlic: page 54
Cooking pasta: page 39

KEYS TO SUCCESS

■ Use a deep, heavy pot so the sauce does not thicken too quickly.

■ Cook the soffritto vegetables slowly over low heat. This is essential to release their full flavor.

■ Don't skimp on the cooking time. This is the secret of a good Bolognese.

■ If there is any excess fat on the top of the sauce at the end, blot it off with paper towels.

INGREDIENTS

SERVES 6

1 small celery stalk, trimmed

1 medium Spanish onion, peeled

1 medium carrot, peeled

2 large garlic cloves, peeled

2 tbsp olive oil

2 tbsp butter

1lb (500g) ground beef

1 tbsp all-purpose flour

3 tbsp tomato paste

½ cup (150ml) beef stock

½ cup (150ml) red wine

14oz (400g) canned chopped tomatoes

nutmeg, salt, and pepper

16oz (500g) tagliatelle

fresh Parmesan

BOLOGNESE SAUCE served with tagliatelle and topped with fresh Parmesan cheese is a traditional Italian favorite.

TAGLIATELLE BOLOGNESE

1 PULL OFF AND DISCARD any tough strings from the back of the celery stalk. Using a chef's knife, finely chop the celery, onion, and carrot. Crush the garlic in a garlic press.

2 POUR THE OIL into a large pot, then add the butter. Put the pot over medium heat until the butter melts and foams. Turn the heat down to low.

5 ADD THE TOMATO PASTE, beef stock, red wine, and tomatoes. Using a nutmeg grater held over the pot, add about 8 gratings of fresh nutmeg. Add salt and pepper.

6 BRING TO A BOIL, stirring constantly, then reduce the heat to very low so that the mixture is just simmering. Partially cover the pot, making sure steam can still escape.

3 ADD THE CELERY, onion, carrot, and garlic to the oil and butter and cook over low heat, stirring constantly, for about 5 minutes, or until softened but not browned.

4 ADD THE MEAT to the softened vegetables, break it up with a wooden spoon, then cook until it loses its redness, stirring frequently. Sprinkle in the flour and stir in well.

7 COOK THE SAUCE for about 1 hour, stirring every 15 minutes or so to check that the mixture is not sticking to the bottom of the pot. If it is, add a little water and stir well.

8 WHEN READY, the sauce will be thick and glossy. Taste to check seasoning. Keep the sauce warm and cook the pasta (see page 39). Pour the sauce over the pasta and mix.

MASTER RECIPE

TECHNIQUES

Trimming chops: page 51
Onions: page 54

COOK'S NOTES

Preparation time
5 minutes to prepare the chops
and grate the onion

Cooking time
About 6 minutes

Special equipment
Deep nonstick sauté pan

Nutritional information
Calories: 646
Total fat: 76g of which
unsaturated fat: 34g
saturated fat: 38g
Sodium: 213mg

Shopping tips
Red-skinned onions are milder
and sweeter than the
brown-skinned varieties, but if
you can't get them, buy
the largest brown-skinned
onions you can find – look for
onions labeled "mild."
As a general rule, the larger
the onion, the milder it will be.

SAUTÉED LAMB CHOPS

Packed with protein, sautéed lamb chops make a perfect meal

for two for an evening at home, and the flavorful sauce

is quick and easy to make from the meat's own

juices. To enjoy the flavor of the lamb chops at their best,

serve them as soon as the sauce is cooked.

KEYS TO SUCCESS

■ Use a heavy nonstick pan – the lamb will then cook in its own juices, and no extra fat will be needed.

■ Never add salt before pan-frying meat; it draws out the juices, which gather on the surface and prevent it from browning properly.

■ The cooking time is for slightly pink lamb; if you prefer it well done, cook for 1–2 minutes longer.

INGREDIENTS

SERVES 2

4 loin lamb chops

salt and pepper

ONION GRAVY

1 small red onion, peeled and grated

⅓ cup (100ml) red wine

1 tsp Dijon mustard

1 tsp honey

SAUTÉED CHOPS
*served with new
potatoes, carrots, and
onion gravy make
a nutritious meal.*

1 TRIM ANY EXCESS FAT from the chops. Heat the nonstick sauté pan over high heat for 2 minutes. Grind pepper over both sides of each chop, then place in the hot pan.

2 REDUCE THE HEAT to medium and set a timer for 3 minutes. When the time is up, turn the chops over and reset the timer for 3 more minutes. Lift out the chops.

3 ADD THE GRATED RED ONION to the juices that are left in the pan. Stir over medium heat for about 4 minutes, then add the wine, mustard, and honey. Stir well to mix.

4 ALLOW TO SIMMER GENTLY for 1 minute until reduced to 5–6 tbsp. Add salt and pepper, stir with a wooden spoon, check seasoning, and serve with the chops.

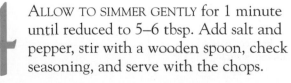

STIR-FRIED GINGER CHICKEN

The art of the stir-fry is to cook finely chopped ingredients swiftly in a small amount of hot oil in a wok. Intense heat ensures ingredients cook in the minimum amount of time, so it is one of the fastest and healthiest methods of cooking. This classic Chinese combination of chicken and ginger is wonderfully aromatic.

COOK'S NOTES

Prepare ahead
The vegetables and chicken can be prepared and kept, covered, in the refrigerator for up to 3 hours

Preparation time
About 15 minutes

Cooking time
4–6 minutes

Special equipment
Large wok
Wok shovel or spatula (two shovels or spatulas make it easier to lift and toss the ingredients thoroughly)

Nutritional information
Calories: 545
Total fat: 21g of which
unsaturated fat: 15g
saturated fat: 4g
Sodium: 1074mg

Shopping tips
Fresh ginger is pungent, almost lemony tasting, with a knobby shape and thin, pale brown skin. You can buy it in varying lengths; simply break off the amount you need. To use, first peel with a vegetable peeler or small knife, then slice into matchsticks or grate on the coarse side of a box grater.

TECHNIQUES

Soaking noodles: page 39
Carrots: page 57
Peppers: page 55
Pounding & slicing chicken: page 51

KEYS TO SUCCESS

■ Cut the ingredients fine, no more than ¼in (5mm) thick and 2in (5cm) long, so that they cook quickly and evenly. Pound chicken and slice it across the grain, to break up fibers.

■ Prepare all the ingredients and assemble them before starting to cook. Once stir-frying starts, the ingredients cook so quickly there is no time for chopping and slicing.

■ If you do not have a wok and a shovel, use a large, deep, nonstick sauté pan instead, and toss the ingredients with a wooden spatula to avoid scratching.

■ The wok should never be more than one third full. The food should have room to touch the hot sides of the wok.

INGREDIENTS

8oz (250g) Chinese egg noodles

3 tbsp peanut oil

6 scallions, sliced on the diagonal into short lengths

1in (2.5cm) piece of fresh ginger, peeled and cut into matchsticks

4 medium carrots, cut into sticks

2 medium peppers (1 red, 1 yellow), cored, seeded, and cut into sticks

¾lb (350g) skinless boneless chicken breasts, pounded and sliced

2 tbsp dry sherry

4 tbsp dark soy sauce

a few fresh cilantro leaves, to garnish

THIS COLORFUL STIR-FRY
makes a quick and easy
one-dish meal.

STIR-FRIED GINGER CHICKEN

1 FIRST SOAK THE NOODLES (see page 39). Place the wok over high heat for 1–2 minutes until very hot. To test the temperature, add a drop of the oil – it will sizzle when the wok is ready.

2 ADD THE REMAINING OIL to the hot wok and swirl the pan to coat the sides. Heat the oil until it just begins to smoke – this happens very quickly, so watch it carefully.

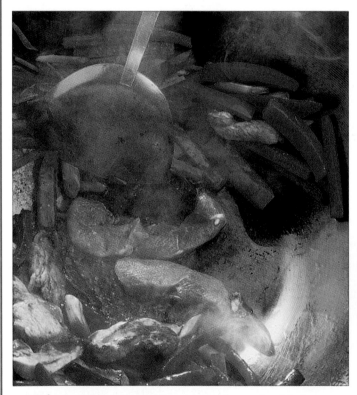

5 PUSH THE VEGETABLES aside and add the chicken a little at a time. Sizzle the chicken briefly on each side before tossing with the other ingredients for 1–2 minutes longer.

6 POUR IN THE SHERRY and allow it to simmer briefly (this burns off the alcohol but maintains flavor). Add the soy sauce and stir to mix with the chicken and vegetables.

3 DROP THE PIECES of scallion and ginger into the hot oil – they will sizzle. Stir them around vigorously with the shovel for about 1 minute, tossing to coat them in the oil.

4 PUSH THE SCALLIONS and ginger to one side. Add the carrots and peppers and stir-fry in the same way for 1–2 minutes, then stir the scallions and ginger back in.

7 DRAIN THE NOODLES (see page 39), add to the wok, and toss to mix. Taste and add more soy sauce if you like. Serve immediately, sprinkled with cilantro leaves.

VARIATIONS

SHRIMP & ASPARAGUS
Omit the carrots, peppers, and chicken. Add ½lb (200g) asparagus, sliced and tough ends removed, in step 4. Add ¾lb (400g) peeled cooked shrimp in step 7 and heat through.

BEEF & SNOW PEAS
Omit the chicken and noodles. Add ¾lb (350g) round steak, pounded and sliced, in step 5; cook as chicken. Add ¼lb (100g) snow peas before the sherry and soy sauce in step 6.

ORIENTAL FISH
Omit the chicken, noodles, carrots, and yellow pepper. Use 2 red peppers, sliced, in step 4. Add ¾lb (350g) skinned cod fillet chunks, with ½lb (250g) napa or bok choy, shredded, in step 5.

MASTER RECIPE

GRILLED SALMON FILLETS

Grilling on top of the stove in a ridged, cast-iron pan is a quick, fun way to cook. Food cooked this way is succulent, full of natural flavor, and low in fat, and with its attractive charred pattern of stripes, it has the added bonus of looking good. In order to achieve perfect results, accurate timing is essential.

COOK'S NOTES

Preparation time
5 minutes

Cooking time
About 6 minutes

Special equipment
Ridged cast-iron grill pan for use on the stovetop: most pans are only big enough for two generous portions, and it is best not to grill more than this or the pan will be overcrowded and the food will not cook properly.
If you do not have this type of pan, you can cook the salmon fillets for the same length of time in a sauté pan or under the broiler.

Nutritional information
Calories: 342
Total fat: 26g of which
unsaturated fat: 19g
saturated fat: 5g
Sodium: 61mg

Serving tips
Lemon wedges make a good accompaniment to salmon fillets

KEYS TO SUCCESS

■ Preheat the pan dry before starting to cook. If oil is added when the pan is empty, it will burn and smoke. To test if the pan is hot enough, sprinkle water over it from your fingertips. It should dance, then quickly disappear.

■ Keep the food in one place during cooking. This will ensure that the ridges leave their characteristic charred pattern on the food.

■ The cooking time given here is for thick pieces of salmon; if you can only buy long, thin salmon fillets, cook for about 2 minutes on each side.

■ After cooking, let the pan cool slightly before soaking it in hot soapy water. If a cast-iron pan is plunged into cold water when it is red-hot, it might crack. You will need a stiff brush to clean between the ridges.

INGREDIENTS

SERVES 2

2 thick pieces of salmon fillet, skin on, about ¼lb (125g) each

2–3 tbsp peanut oil

salt and pepper

GRILLED SALMON served with boiled new potatoes and snow peas is a healthy main course.

TECHNIQUES

Preparing salmon: page 43

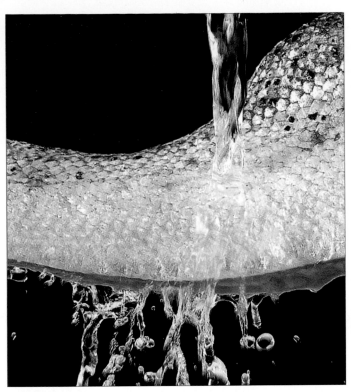

1 REMOVE ANY TINY PIN BONES from the salmon fillets, trim, rinse, and pat dry (see page 43). Preheat the grill pan over high heat for about 10 minutes.

2 WHILE THE PAN is heating on the burner, brush both sides of the salmon fillets with peanut oil, then sprinkle them liberally with salt and pepper.

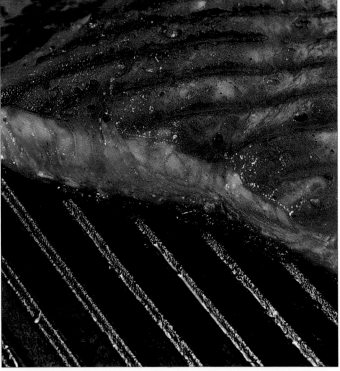

3 REDUCE THE HEAT to medium. Place the salmon, skin side up, on the hot pan and set a timer for 3 minutes. When the time is up, carefully turn the fish over using a spatula.

4 RESET THE TIMER for 3 more minutes and continue cooking. Check to see whether the fish is opaque all along the cut edges. If not, cook for a few seconds longer.

MASTER RECIPE

BROILED VEGETABLE KEBABS

Broiling browns food quickly on the outside while concentrating and sealing the juices in the center. This gives broiled food its distinctive charred taste. Marinating adds extra flavor and moisture, which is particularly important when cooking quickly by dry heat.

COOK'S NOTES

Preparation time
5 minutes for the marinade
15 minutes for the vegetables
1–4 hours to marinate

Cooking time
8–10 minutes

Special equipment
Eight skewers. Metal, flat-bladed skewers are best, but if you only have wooden ones, soak them in warm water for about 30 minutes before use to keep them from burning under the broiler.

Nutritional information
Calories: 403
Total fat: 27g of which
unsaturated fat: 15g
saturated fat: 10g
Sodium: 456mg

Shopping tips
Halloumi is a semisoft Greek cheese. Its slightly rubbery texture is ideal for broiling since it holds its shape well. Mildly salty, the cheese should be rinsed with water before use. If you use mozzarella, choose the Danish type that is sold in shrink-wrapped blocks. The round Italian kind is too soft to stay on the skewers during broiling.

TECHNIQUES

Peppers: page 55
Onions: page 54
Zucchini: page 56
Mushrooms: page 57
Chopping herbs: page 71
Garlic: page 54

KEYS TO SUCCESS

■ Make sure the vegetables and cheese are cut into even-sized chunks so they will all cook at the same rate.

■ Preheat the broiler and move the food around often during cooking to counter the effect of broiler hot spots.

INGREDIENTS

2 large peppers (1 red, 1 green)

1 large Spanish onion

2 medium zucchini

16 large commercial mushrooms

8 ears baby corn

½lb (250g) halloumi or mozzarella cheese

6 tbsp (90ml) olive oil

1 tbsp wine vinegar

3 tbsp chopped mixed fresh herbs

2 large garlic cloves, peeled and finely chopped or crushed

salt and pepper

VEGETABLE KEBABS
*served with couscous
make a light and
colorful vegetarian
main dish.*

94

1 CORE THE PEPPERS, peel the onion, and trim the zucchini (see pages 54–56). Chop them into 1in (2.5cm) chunks. Leave the mushrooms and corn whole. Cut the cheese into chunks.

2 MIX THE OLIVE OIL, vinegar, herbs, and garlic in a large bowl. Add the vegetables, cheese and salt and pepper, then stir to coat in the marinade. Cover and chill for 1–4 hours.

3 LIFT THE VEGETABLES and cheese out of the marinade. Thread them onto eight skewers, mixing the cheese and vegetables evenly. Preheat the broiler for 5 minutes on high.

4 REDUCE THE HEAT to medium-high, brush broiler rack with oil, and arrange skewers on top. Broil, about 4in (10cm) from the heat, for 8–10 minutes, turning twice.

MASTER RECIPE

CHILI CON CARNE

There are many different chili recipes. This is a good basic one that combines both fresh chilies and chili powder for a unique taste. Be cautious when adding any kind of chili or powder as it is always difficult to estimate the heat. If you think the sauce needs spicing up at the end of cooking, add a few drops of Tabasco.

COOK'S NOTES

Prepare ahead
Chili con carne benefits from being made ahead – the cooling and reheating process improves its flavor. After cooling, keep covered in the refrigerator for up to 3 days. It can also be frozen for up to 3 months.

Preparation time
Overnight soaking for dried beans
20 minutes to prepare the remaining ingredients

Cooking time
About 1¼ hours for dried beans
About 2½ hours for the main dish

Special equipment
Medium saucepan
Large saucepan

Nutritional information
Calories: 577
Total fat: 23g of which
unsaturated fat: 14g
saturated fat: 7g
Sodium: 628mg

Serving tips
For extra variety, serve with bowls of grated Cheddar cheese, sour cream, chopped raw onion, chopped fresh cilantro, salsa, and diced avocado. Tortilla chips or fresh tortillas can also be served as an accompaniment.

TECHNIQUES

Dried beans: page 41
Trimming meat: page 51
Onions: page 54
Garlic: page 54
Chilies: page 55
Peppers: page 55

KEYS TO SUCCESS

■ For a quicker chili, use two 14oz (400g) cans red kidney beans, drained and rinsed; add with peppers in step 6.

■ Browning the meat is important. Add the meat a few pieces at a time, leaving some space around each piece. If all of the meat is put into the pan at the same time, the temperature will be lowered, leaving insufficient heat to seal the meat.

■ Cook the chili for a long time at a low oven temperature. This allows the meat to develop a tender, moist texture and a mellow flavor. If the temperature is too high, the meat will cook too quickly and be chewy.

INGREDIENTS

1¼ cups (225g) dried red kidney beans

1½lb (700g) braising steak, cubed

2 tbsp sunflower oil

2 medium onions, peeled and finely chopped

1 garlic clove, peeled and crushed

1–2 fresh chilies, seeded and thinly sliced

3 tbsp all-purpose flour

1 tbsp chili powder

14oz (400g) canned chopped tomatoes

2 tbsp tomato paste

1¾ cups (425ml) water

1 beef bouillon cube, crumbled

1 large red pepper, cored, seeded, diced

salt and pepper

CHILI CON CARNE *served with plain boiled rice makes a good party dish.*

CHILI CON CARNE

1 SOAK THE DRIED BEANS. Boil for 10 minutes, then cook for 1½ hours (see page 41) and drain. Rinse in cold running water; set aside. Preheat the oven to 300°F (150°C).

2 TRIM THE FAT from the meat. Pour half the oil into a medium saucepan and heat over medium heat until a haze appears. Add about one quarter of the meat, spacing chunks out.

5 ADD THE FLOUR and chili powder and stir for 3–4 minutes. Add the beans, tomatoes, and meat with its juices, then the tomato paste, water, and bouillon cube.

6 STIR UNTIL JUST SIMMERING, season, cover, and transfer to the oven. Cook for 1½ hours, then add the diced pepper. Re-cover and return to the oven for 30 minutes longer.

3 COOK OVER HIGH HEAT for 2–3 minutes before turning, then keep turning until brown all over. Using a slotted spoon, transfer the cubes to a plate. Repeat with the remaining meat.

4 ADD THE REMAINING OIL to the pan, heat over medium heat for 1 minute, and then add the onions, garlic, and chilies. Cook for 3 minutes, stirring to loosen the residue from the bottom.

7 BEFORE SERVING, test a piece of the meat and a few of the beans by biting into them to make sure they are tender. Taste the sauce to check the seasoning.

VEGETARIAN CHILI

1 Use 1½lb (700g) chopped mixed vegetables instead of the beef and two 14oz (400g) cans red kidney beans. Suitable vegetables to use include broccoli, peppers, eggplant, and zucchini.

2 Cook the vegetables with the onions, garlic, and chilies in the sunflower oil until soft and lightly browned. Sprinkle in the flour and chili powder and cook as in step 5 of the main recipe.

3 Drain and rinse the red kidney beans. Add to pan with tomatoes, tomato paste, water, a crumbled vegetable bouillon cube, and seasoning. Cook, uncovered, over low heat for 45 minutes.

ROAST CHICKEN WITH HERB BUTTER

This is the simplest of roasts, yet easily one of the most popular.

You can serve the bird on a large platter and carve it at

the table or, if you prefer, carve it in the kitchen and arrange slices

on warmed plates. Serve dishes of vegetables separately,

with a gravy boat of piping hot, real homemade gravy.

COOK'S NOTES

Prepare ahead
The chicken can be prepared and spread with the herb butter in advance. Keep it, covered with foil, in the refrigerator for 8–12 hours. Let it stand at room temperature for about 30 minutes before roasting.

Preparation time
10 minutes for the herb butter
15 minutes to prepare the bird
5 minutes for the gravy

Cooking time
1¼–1½ hours, plus 15 minutes resting time

Tools
Roasting pan with hinged V-shaped rack to cradle the bird. If you have a flat rack, prop the bird first on one side of its breast and roast for 20 minutes, then on the other side for 20 minutes. Roast it breast side up for the last part of the roasting time.

Nutritional information
Calories: 662
Total fat: 49g of which
unsaturated fat: 26g
saturated fat: 20g
Sodium: 390mg

TECHNIQUES
Preparing chicken: page 47
Chopping and snipping
herbs: page 71
Squeezing lemon juice: page 64
Carving chicken: page 48

KEYS TO SUCCESS

■ Defrost a frozen bird thoroughly before you prepare it, or it will not cook thoroughly. Pierce the wrapping, then stand the bird on paper towels in a container. Let stand in a cold place overnight (in the refrigerator it will take 36 hours) until no ice crystals remain in the cavity.

■ For the skin to be crisp, it must be completely dry before cooking, so wipe it well with paper towels. This is especially important if the bird has been frozen, because it is often quite wet after defrosting.

■ If the breast skin shows signs of overbrowning during roasting, remove the chicken from the oven, cover it with a "tent" of foil, and then return it to the oven.

INGREDIENTS

3–4lb (1.5–1.8kg) chicken

1 medium onion, unpeeled and cut lengthwise into sections

4 tbsp dry white wine

HERB BUTTER

6 tbsp (85g) butter, at room temperature

3 tbsp finely chopped fresh parsley

1 tbsp finely snipped chives or finely chopped scallion

1 tsp finely chopped fresh tarragon or thyme leaves

1 tsp lemon juice

salt and pepper

ROAST CHICKEN with simply cooked fresh vegetables and real homemade gravy makes a tasty meal that is always popular.

ROAST CHICKEN WITH HERB BUTTER

1 FIRST MAKE THE HERB BUTTER. Put the butter in a bowl and beat it with a wooden spoon to soften it. Add the chopped herbs, scallion if using, lemon juice, and salt and pepper.

2 STIR THE INGREDIENTS together, then beat them vigorously until they are evenly combined. Preheat the oven to 400°F (200°C).

5 TURN THE CHICKEN UPSIDE DOWN and roast for about 20 minutes or until browned, then turn it over so that it is breast side up and baste it with the buttery cooking juices.

6 RETURN THE CHICKEN to the oven and roast for 55–70 minutes more, or until the juices run clear when the flesh is pierced with a knife between the body and a leg.

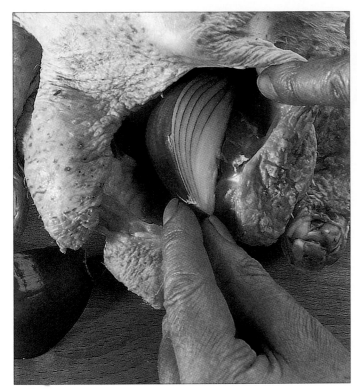

3 PREPARE THE CHICKEN (see page 47), putting two onion sections in the cavity of the bird before tying the legs with string. Put the remaining onion in the roasting pan.

4 PUT THE RACK in the pan and place the bird on the rack. Spread the herb butter liberally all over the bird, then spoon the white wine into the pan.

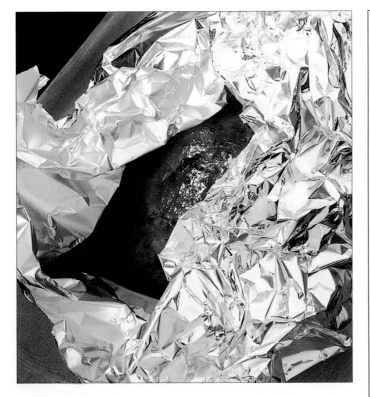

7 WRAP THE CHICKEN in a large sheet of foil, then let it rest for about 15 minutes. Remove the rack and onion from the pan and make the gravy (see right).

MAKING GRAVY

1 Tilt the roasting pan so the juices settle in one corner, then spoon off most of the fat, leaving the dark juices in the pan. Discard the surplus fat. Put the roasting pan on the burner, over medium heat.

2 Sprinkle 2 tsp all-purpose flour over the juices in the pan and whisk with a coil whisk over medium heat for 2–3 minutes until the flour browns a little.

3 Pour in 1¼ cups (300ml) hot stock and bring to the boil, whisking all the time. If you like, add 4 tbsp white or red wine; whisk to mix. Simmer for 2 minutes, then check the seasoning. Makes 1¼ cups (300ml).

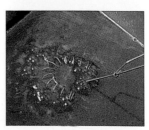

MASTER RECIPE

DOUBLE-CRUST APPLE PIE

Homey and traditional, apple pie is the perfect dessert for a special meal. It never fails to please and is easily within the scope of the new cook. The trick is to have crisp, golden pastry on the outside and tender, juicy fruit that holds its shape on the inside.

COOK'S NOTES

Prepare ahead
The pastry dough can be kept, wrapped in plastic wrap, for up to 24 hours in the refrigerator

Preparation time
10 minutes to make the pastry
30 minutes to chill the pastry
10 minutes for the filling
15 minutes to assemble the pie

Cooking time
About 45 minutes

Special equipment
9in (23cm) pie pan
baking sheet

Nutritional information
Calories: 546
Total fat: 25g of which
unsaturated fat: 13g
saturated fat: 11g
Sodium: 241mg

Taste tips
You can use sweet or tart cooking apples for this pie. McIntosh and Granny Smiths are very good cooking apples for pies. Cooking apples tend to turn brown more quickly than dessert apples. Sprinkling the apples with lemon juice as you slice them helps prevent them from browning and adds to the flavor of the pie. Cooking apples are not as sweet as dessert apples, so always offer extra sugar at the table.

TECHNIQUES
Shortcrust pastry: page 66
Slicing apples: page 62
Squeezing lemon juice: page 64

KEYS TO SUCCESS

■ For crisp, light pastry, always work in a cool kitchen, with cool ingredients and tools.

■ When rolling out the pastry dough, take care not to stretch it because this will cause it to shrink during baking.

■ Use only the amount of sugar specified and serve extra at the table if necessary. Sugar draws out the juice from fruit, and if there is too much, it may overflow during baking. Juice that overflows will stick on the bottom of

your oven. Cornstarch is added to absorb excess juice.

■ Put a baking sheet in the oven while it preheats, then set the pie pan on the sheet to cook, to give crisp pastry and to catch dripping juice.

■ Start cooking the pie at a high temperature to brown the pastry, then reduce the heat to finish cooking the filling at a lower temperature.

INGREDIENTS

6 SLICES

2¾ cups (350g) all-purpose flour

¾ cup (175g) margarine

about 6 tbsp (90ml) cold water

2lb (1kg) apples

juice of 1 small lemon

6 tbsp (85g) granulated sugar

1½ tbsp cornstarch

GLAZE

1 tbsp milk

1 tbsp granulated sugar

SERVED WITH WHIPPED CREAM, ice cream, or cheese, homemade apple pie is the perfect end to any meal.

DOUBLE-CRUST APPLE PIE *Making the pastry and lining the pan*

MAKING THE SHORTCRUST PASTRY

1 Place the flour in a large bowl. Cut the margarine into cubes and add these to the flour.

2 Cut the margarine into the flour with your fingertips until it resembles bread crumbs.

3 Add the water and mix with a knife until the mixture just begins to hold together.

4 Using one hand, gather the mixture together into a rough ball against the side of the bowl.

1 MAKE THE PASTRY as shown left (for more detailed instructions, see page 66). Wrap the ball of pastry in plastic wrap and place in the refrigerator to chill for 30 minutes.

4 BETWEEN EACH ROLLING, turn the pastry a quarter turn, and dust the rolling pin with more flour if it starts to become sticky. Do not stretch the pastry or turn it over.

5 WITH FLOURED HANDS, fold the circle of pastry dough in half, then in half again, to resemble a fan shape. This will make it easier to lift into the pan.

2 LIGHTLY FLOUR the work surface. Unwrap the pastry and cut it in half. Rewrap one piece to prevent it drying out. Gently shape the other half into a smooth ball.

3 FLOUR YOUR ROLLING pin and flatten the pastry. Working the rolling pin from the center outward, roll out the pastry into a circle, about ¼in (5mm) in thickness.

6 BRUSH THE PIE PAN with melted margarine. Place the pastry fan in the pan with the point in the center. This ensures that the pastry is centered and will minimize stretching.

7 UNFOLD THE PASTRY and ease it into the pan without stretching or pulling it. Do not worry about the pastry hanging over the edge because this will be trimmed later.

DOUBLE-CRUST APPLE PIE *Making the filling and finishing the pie*

1 PLACE A BAKING SHEET in the oven and preheat to 425°F (220°C). Quarter, core, and peel apples. Slice them, toss with the lemon juice, then with the sugar and cornstarch.

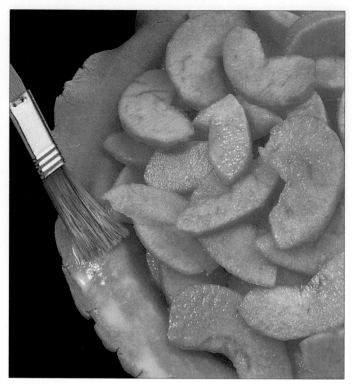

2 PUT THE APPLES into the lined pan. Then use a fork to distribute the slices, heaping them up toward the center. Brush the rim of the pastry with a little milk.

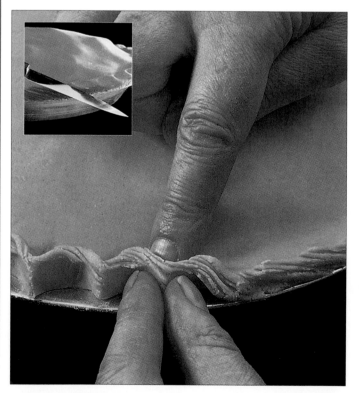

5 EDGE THE PIE by making shallow cuts with the back of a knife (see inset). Flute the edge with your fingertips, then brush the top with milk. Cut a ½in (1cm) steam hole in the center.

6 REROLL THE TRIMMINGS, cut out decorative shapes (see inset), and arrange on top of the pie, leaving the steam hole open. Brush shapes with milk and sift sugar over the pie.

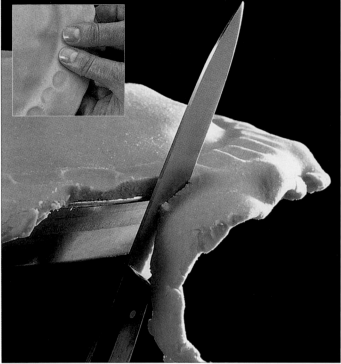

3 UNWRAP AND ROLL OUT the remaining piece of pastry to about the same diameter as the first. Fold into a fan shape as before. Put the point of the fan on the center of the pie.

4 UNFOLD THE PASTRY over the filling and gently press the edge with your thumb tips. Hold the pan in one hand and cut off the excess, holding the knife at a slight angle.

VARIATIONS

RHUBARB & ORANGE
Omit the apples and lemon juice. Trim 2lb (1kg) rhubarb, pull off stringy fibers, and chop into 1in (2.5cm) lengths. Mix zested rind of 1 orange with sugar and cornstarch in step 1.

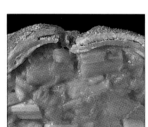

DUTCH APPLE
Use the same amounts of all the ingredients as in the main recipe. Add 1 tsp ground cinnamon to the sugar and cornstarch in step 1; add ½ cup (85g) golden raisins with apples.

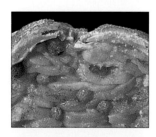

PEACH & ALMOND
Omit the apples and lemon juice. Drain 28oz (400g) canned peaches in natural juice. Toss with the sugar and cornstarch plus ½ tsp almond extract at the end of step 1.

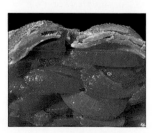

7 BAKE FOR 15 minutes, then turn the oven down to 350°F (180°C) and bake for 30–35 minutes. The pastry should be golden and the filling soft when pierced.

MASTER RECIPE

WHITE LAYER CAKE

There are some very good store-bought cakes available, but once you have made your own you may never want to buy one again. Not only will a home-baked cake taste fresher and better than a purchased one, it will also fill your kitchen with an irresistible aroma.

COOK'S NOTES

Prepare ahead
The cake is best made and eaten on the same day, but it will keep fresh if it is kept in an airtight container for 1–2 days. It can also be frozen for up to 3 months: freeze the unfilled layers separately, leaving the papers on. Wrap each layer in foil and slip into a freezer bag.

Preparation time
10 minutes to line the pans and make the cake mixture
5 minutes to assemble and sprinkle with sugar after baking

Cooking time
20–30 minutes

Special equipment
2 x 8in (20cm) loose-bottomed layer cake pans
Electric mixer

Nutritional information
Calories: 511
Total fat: 27g of which
unsaturated fat: 17g
saturated fat: 8g
Sodium: 513mg

Shopping tips
If you are in a hurry, you can save time by using precut circles of waxed paper or nonstick baking parchment, available from specialty shops and the kitchenware sections of department stores. They are also sold by mail order.

TECHNIQUES
Cracking eggs: page 34

KEYS TO SUCCESS

■ When lining the cake pans, remove the base of each pan and draw around each one on waxed paper or nonstick baking parchment. Cut out circles from the paper and grease the base and sides of each pan well. The pans must be greased evenly, or the cakes will not rise properly.

■ Soft margarine, sold in cups, blends easily for this all-in-one method. It must be used straight from the refrigerator. Do not use low-fat spread because its water content is too high and it will spoil the result.

■ Together, the baking powder and self-rising flour give the cake an extra lift, so there is no need for endless beating. Here an electric mixer is used, but you can get good results with a wooden spoon if the margarine is at room temperature.

■ The baking time is only a guide. Look at the cake after the minimum time. If it is golden but soft in the center, lay a sheet of foil over it and cook for an extra 5–10 minutes.

INGREDIENTS

6 GENEROUS SLICES

12 tbsp (175g) margarine

¾ cup (175g) superfine sugar

1½ cups (175g) self-rising flour

1½ tsp baking powder

3 large eggs

FILLING & TOPPING

about 4 tbsp raspberry or strawberry jam

a little superfine sugar

FILLED WITH JAM *and dusted with sugar, this layer cake is one of the quickest and easiest you can make.*

WHITE LAYER CAKE

1 PREHEAT THE OVEN to 350°F (180°C). Cut 2 waxed-paper circles, grease the cake pans with margarine, and put the circles inside. Grease the circles once in the pans with margarine.

2 PLACE THE MARGARINE in a large mixing bowl, then add the superfine sugar, self-rising flour, and baking powder. Crack the eggs one at a time and then add to the bowl.

5 THE CAKES ARE READY when they have risen and are pale golden. The tops should spring back when lightly pressed. Cool for about 2 minutes; loosen the edges with a knife.

6 PUSH THE CAKES out of the pans on their bases, invert them, and remove the bases. Cool the cakes right side up on a rack. Soften the jam with a palette knife.

3 USING AN ELECTRIC MIXER on slow, beat for 2 minutes, or until smooth. The mixture will be soft enough to drop off the beaters when you lift them up.

4 DIVIDE THE MIXTURE equally between the prepared pans and level the surfaces with a narrow spatula or a butter knife. Place in oven and bake for 20–30 minutes.

VARIATIONS

LEMON-CREAM CAKE
Add the zested rind of 1 lemon in step 2. For the filling, whip ⅔ cup (150ml) heavy cream until thick, then stir in 4 tbsp lemon curd.

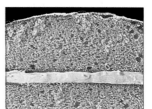

CHOCOLATE CAKE
Mix 2 tbsp cocoa powder with 3 tbsp boiling water. Add to mixture before beating. For filling, melt 5oz (140g) semisweet chocolate with ⅔ cup (150ml) heavy cream. Let cool.

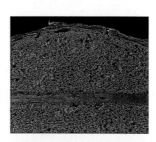

ICED LIME CAKE
Add zested rind of 2 limes in step 2. Use 4 tbsp lime marmalade for filling. Mix 1 cup (100g) confectioners' sugar with enough lime juice to give a creamy texture; spoon over cake.

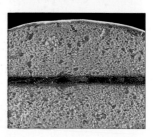

7 WHEN THE CAKES are cold, remove the lining papers and invert one cake layer onto a plate. Spread with jam, put the other layer on top, and sprinkle with superfine sugar.

THREE-SEED CROWN LOAF

Even if you have never made bread before, this simple recipe will enable you to make a loaf to be proud of the first time that you try. It uses instant yeast, which is much easier for a new cook to deal with than fresh yeast – and a little quicker, too.

COOK'S NOTES

Prepare ahead
The dough can be made the day before. After covering the bowl with plastic wrap, place it in the refrigerator overnight. Remove it from the refrigerator and let stand until it doubles in size, then continue from step 6.

Preparation time
15 minutes to mix and knead
2–2½ hours rising

Cooking time
About 30 minutes

Special equipment
8 in (20cm) springform or loose-bottomed pan

Nutritional information
Calories: 265
Total fat: 9g of which
unsaturated fat: 7g
saturated fat: 1g
Sodium: 393mg

Taste tips
Unbleached white flour can be substituted for half the whole-wheat flour to give a lighter-textured result. The toppings can be varied according to what you have on hand. Rolled oats or caraway seeds could be used instead of the seeds suggested here.

KEYS TO SUCCESS

■ Most important is to use bread flour, which is made especially for the purpose. It has a high gluten content, which makes the dough elastic.

■ Take care that the water is lukewarm, not too hot or it will kill the yeast. If you mix half boiling and half cold water, it will be the right temperature.

■ Knead dough thoroughly, either by hand or using a food processor with a dough blade. Dough should be sticky; if it is too dry, your bread will be dry.

■ Bread will rise at any temperature, but the colder the dough the longer it takes. A suitable temperature is 75°F (25°C); good places for rising include an unlit gas oven or a warm kitchen.

■ A hot oven is crucial, so make sure the oven is preheated to the correct temperature: 450°F (230°C).

■ Make sure the loaf is cooked before cooling. Remove it from its pan and tap it on the bottom, it should sound hollow. If not, place upside-down in the oven for a few minutes more.

INGREDIENTS

MAKES AN 8IN (20CM) LOAF MADE UP OF 8 ROLLS

4 cups (500g) unbleached whole-wheat flour

2 tsp salt

1 envelope instant yeast

1¼ cups (300ml) lukewarm water

2 tbsp honey

2 tbsp plus 1 tsp sunflower oil

¾ cup (125g) sunflower seeds

2 tbsp poppy seeds

2 tbsp sesame seeds

SEEDED ROLLS look good sliced and served with butter and cheese.

THREE-SEED CROWN LOAF

1 MEASURE THE FLOUR, salt, and yeast into a large bowl. Measure the water in a cup, then stir in the honey and 2 tbsp sunflower oil. Pour the liquid into the dry ingredients.

2 MIX TO FORM a soft dough. The dough should be wet enough to cling to the bowl: add more lukewarm water if necessary. Scrape the dough out onto a lightly floured surface.

5 TURN THE DOUGH in the oil, then cover the bowl with plastic wrap. Let the dough stand in a warm place for about 1½ hours or until it has doubled in size.

6 TURN OUT DOUGH and pat flat. Scatter with ½ cup (100g) of the sunflower seeds, then roll up and knead for 20–30 turns. Shape into a round, cut into 8 wedges, then roll into balls.

3 KNEAD THE DOUGH for 10 minutes. To knead, use the weight of your body to push down with the heel of your hand into the dough and then stretch it out away from your body.

4 FOLD THE END of the dough back to the top. Give the dough a quarter turn and repeat, building up a smooth rocking action. Rub the teaspoon of oil around a large bowl.

7 DIP 3 BALLS in poppy seeds, 2 in sesame, 2 in sunflower, 1 in whole-wheat flour. Grease the pan. Place the balls inside and let rise for 35–40 minutes. Preheat oven (see page 114).

8 BAKE FOR 10 MINUTES. Lower the heat to 400°F (200°C) for 20 minutes longer. Release the springform catch, remove the bread from the pan, and test. Cool on a rack.

EVERY COOK needs a collection of tried-and-true recipes to turn to, and this chapter provides just that. Here you will find a wide range of dishes – everyday soups; eggs and pasta; main-course fish, poultry, and meat dishes; vegetarian meals and vegetable side dishes; favorite desserts; even snacktime treats like muffins and brownies. All of the recipes are easy, based on the skills shown in the Master Recipes, so you can be sure of success every time. As you cook more and more of these recipes, your confidence will let you experiment with ideas of your own, and you will develop a personal culinary style.

RECIPE REPERTOIRE

EGG DISHES

For suppers and snacks, first courses and light lunches, eggs make

quick, nutritious meals. The recipes in this section

are all straightforward, based on simple cooking techniques.

QUICHE LORRAINE

6–8 thick bacon slices, diced

*8in (20cm) pastry shell, baked
empty and left in pan
(see pages 66–67)*

*1 medium onion, peeled
and chopped*

*¼lb (125g) Gruyère
cheese, grated*

2 large eggs

1 cup (250ml) light cream

salt and pepper

saturated fat 26g • unsaturated fat 25g
sodium 1012mg • calories 742

1 Preheat oven to 350°F (180°C).
Crisp the bacon in a nonstick
sauté pan over medium heat for 10
minutes. Lift out and transfer to
pastry shell. Leave juices in pan.

2 Put the onion in the pan and
cook over medium heat for
8 minutes, or until golden. Add to
the quiche; top with the cheese.

3 Mix the eggs, cream, and salt
and pepper, then pour into the
quiche. Bake for 25–30 minutes,
until golden and set. Serve warm.

SPINACH &
MUSHROOM QUICHE

¾lb (300g) fresh young spinach

3 tbsp butter

*6oz (200g) mushrooms,
trimmed and sliced*

*1 large garlic clove, peeled
and crushed*

2 large eggs

1 cup (250ml) light cream

2 tsp lemon juice

salt and pepper

*8in (20cm) pastry shell, baked
empty and left in pan
(see pages 66–67)*

saturated fat 22g • unsaturated fat 19g
sodium 433mg • calories 579

1 Preheat the oven to 350°F
(180°C). Put the spinach and
half the butter in a large nonstick
sauté pan. Stir-fry over high heat
for a few minutes until the spinach
is wilted. Transfer to a bowl and
let cool.

2 Melt the remaining butter in
the same pan and add the
mushrooms and garlic. Stir-fry
over medium-high heat for
3–5 minutes, or until the
moisture has evaporated. Add to
the spinach and let cool.

3 Mix the eggs, cream, and
lemon juice in a large bowl.
Add the spinach, mushrooms,
and salt and pepper, then pour
into the pastry shell. Bake for
25–30 minutes, until golden and
set. Serve warm.

CRACKING & SEPARATING EGGS

Always try to break the egg in the middle, so the two halves are
even. For more detailed information, see pages 34–36.

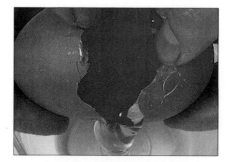

*To crack open shell, tap the middle on
the rim of a bowl and pry it apart.*

*To separate white from yolk, crack egg
in half and tilt to pour white out.*

CHEESE SOUFFLÉS

If you prefer, you can make 1 large soufflé in a 2½ cup (600ml) soufflé dish. Bake for about 30 minutes.

3 tbsp butter

⅓ cup (40g) all-purpose flour

1¼ cups (300ml) hot milk

1¼ cups (150g) grated aged Cheddar cheese

1 tsp Dijon mustard

salt and pepper

4 large eggs, separated

*saturated fat 18g • unsaturated fat 12g
sodium 496mg • calories 409*

1 Preheat the oven to 350°F (180°C). Brush the insides of four ⅔ cup (150ml) ramekins with butter.

2 Melt the butter in a saucepan over medium heat, sprinkle in the flour, and whisk for 1–2 minutes. Remove from the heat and gradually add the hot milk, whisking constantly. Return to medium heat and continue whisking until the sauce is boiling and thickened. Remove from the heat, then add the cheese and stir until melted. Add the mustard and salt and pepper.

3 Let the sauce cool a little, then beat in the egg yolks. Whisk the egg whites in a large bowl with an electric mixer until stiff. Whisk 2 heaping tbsp whites into the sauce, then gently fold in the remainder.

4 Spoon the mixture into the ramekins. Bake for about 15 minutes, or until risen and golden brown. Serve immediately.

CREPES SUZETTE

8 x 6in (16cm) thin crepes (see page 37)

4 tbsp orange liqueur or brandy

FOR THE SAUCE

juice of 2 oranges

½ cup (125g) unsalted butter

⅓ cup (60g) superfine sugar

*saturated fat 19g • unsaturated fat 11g
sodium 60mg • calories 489*

1 First make the sauce: put the orange juice, butter, and sugar in a large nonstick sauté pan. Stir over medium heat until the butter has melted, then simmer gently for 5 minutes.

2 Reduce the heat to low. Place 1 crepe in the pan and turn it over to coat with sauce on both sides. Fold it in half, then in half again. Move to the side of pan.

3 Add another crepe, coat it with sauce, and fold. Move it to overlap the first crepe, then repeat with the remaining crepes.

4 Spoon the liqueur or brandy over the crepes in the pan and serve immediately.

APPLE-STUFFED CREPES

4 tbsp unsalted butter

zest of 1 lemon

juice of ½ lemon

1lb (500g) apples

¼ cup (50g) light brown sugar

8 x 9in (23cm) thin crepes (see page 37)

*saturated fat 11g • unsaturated fat 7g
sodium 53mg • calories 336*

1 Melt 2 tbsp of the butter in a large nonstick sauté pan over low heat. Add the lemon zest and juice, stir to mix, then remove from the heat.

2 Quarter, core, and peel the apples, then thickly slice them into the lemon butter. Toss to coat in the mixture.

3 Return the pan to low heat, cover, and continue to cook for 5–10 minutes, or until the apples are just tender but still holding their shape. Remove from the heat. Add half the sugar and stir gently.

4 Preheat the oven to 400°F (200°C). Divide the apple filling among the crepes. Fold the edges of each crepe in over the filling to make a square. Arrange the crepes, seam side down, in a buttered baking dish.

5 Melt the remaining butter and brush over the crepes, then sprinkle over the remaining light brown sugar. Bake the crepes, uncovered, for 20 minutes, or until piping hot. Serve hot, with vanilla ice cream or fresh cream.

SPANISH OMELET

This thick potato omelet is called *tortilla* in Spanish.

1lb (500g) medium to large potatoes, peeled

1 large Spanish onion, peeled and roughly chopped

salt and pepper

5 tbsp (75ml) olive oil

5 large eggs, beaten

saturated fat 5g • unsaturated fat 21g
sodium 113mg • calories 370

1 Using the slicing disk on a food processor, or a chef's knife, cut the potatoes into slices ¼in (5mm) thick. Place the slices in a large bowl and add the onion and salt and pepper. Toss together so they are well mixed.

2 Heat 3 tbsp of the oil in a 9in (23cm) nonstick omelet pan. Add the potatoes and onions, spread them out, then cover with a lid or a sheet of foil. Cook over low heat, stirring occasionally, for about 15 minutes, or until soft but not browned.

3 Add the remaining oil to the pan and turn up the heat to medium. Pour in the beaten eggs, add salt and pepper, and shake to spread the eggs evenly.

4 Cook for about 10 minutes, or until the omelet is set on the bottom but still a little runny on top. Meanwhile, preheat the broiler to medium-high.

5 Put the pan under the broiler and cook for 1–2 minutes, or until the top is set and golden brown. Serve hot, warm, or cold.

ITALIAN HERB FRITTATA

A *frittata* is a baked omelet. Make sure your omelet pan fits in the oven and is ovenproof. Protect the handle with foil, if necessary.

8 large eggs

⅔ cup (150ml) light cream

½ cup (50g) grated Cheddar cheese

¼ cup (25g) grated Parmesan cheese

2 tbsp chopped fresh herbs

salt and pepper

2 tbsp olive oil

saturated fat 13g • unsaturated fat 19g
sodium 339mg • calories 400

1 Preheat the oven to 350°F (180°C). Beat the eggs with the cream, cheeses, herbs, and salt and pepper.

2 Heat the oil in a 9in (23cm) nonstick omelet pan over medium heat until hot. Pour in the egg mixture and shake to spread the ingredients evenly.

3 Transfer to the oven and bake for 20 minutes, or until the omelet is just set in the center.

4 Hold a warmed plate upside down over the pan and turn the two over together so the omelet inverts onto the plate. Serve hot or warm.

EGG MAYONNAISE WITH HERBS

This is a low-fat version of a classic recipe. The sauce can be prepared up to 3 hours ahead and kept in the refrigerator.

6 large eggs

2 bunches arugula leaves

1–2 tbsp French dressing (see page 69)

FOR THE SAUCE

¾ cup (200ml) low-fat crème fraîche or low-fat plain yogurt

¾ cup (200ml) reduced-calorie mayonnaise

1 tbsp lemon juice

½ tsp superfine sugar

1 tbsp each finely chopped parsley, mint, basil, and tarragon

salt and pepper

saturated fat 5g • unsaturated fat 24g
sodium 643mg • calories 364

1 First make the sauce: mix together all the sauce ingredients, then taste to check the seasoning. Cover and chill.

2 Hard boil, peel, and cool the eggs, then drain and dry them. Cut each egg lengthwise in half.

3 Just before serving, arrange the arugula leaves on a serving plate and spoon the French dressing evenly over them.

4 Place the egg halves, cut side down, in a clover-leaf pattern, on top of the arugula. Spoon the sauce over them. Serve 3 egg halves per person.

SCRAMBLED EGGS WITH SPICY PEPPERS

4 tbsp olive oil

1 large Spanish onion, peeled and chopped

3 medium peppers (any color), cored, seeded, and thinly sliced

2 garlic cloves, peeled and crushed

½ small fresh chili, seeded and finely chopped

8 large eggs

salt and pepper

4 medium tomatoes, halved, seeded, and chopped

saturated fat 6g • unsaturated fat 21g sodium 180mg • calories 376

1 Heat 2 tbsp of the oil in a saucepan. Add the onion and cook over medium heat for about 5 minutes. Add the peppers, garlic, and chili and stir to mix. Cover and cook over low heat for 10 minutes, or until all the vegetables are softened.

2 Meanwhile, crack the eggs and place in a large bowl, add salt and pepper, and mix well with a fork. Heat the remaining 2 tbsp oil in an 8in (20cm) nonstick sauté pan over low heat. Pour in the eggs.

3 Cook for 3 minutes, or until very softly scrambled. Stir and scrape all around the bottom of the pan as the egg mixture cooks. Do not overcook – scrambled eggs should be creamy, not set.

4 Add the tomatoes to the spicy pepper mixture, then check the seasoning. Spoon this mixture over the scrambled eggs. Serve immediately.

SOUPS

These soups – some light and smooth, some chunky and

substantial – are all easy to make. They can be

served as a first course, or as a main meal with bread.

PURÉEING SOUPS

Instructions are given in the following three soup recipes for puréeing with an electric handheld blender. If you don't have one of these, use a food processor or a freestanding blender, but cool the soup slightly first and purée it in batches.

If you have none of these, pour the soup into a sieve set over a bowl and press the solids through with the back of a spoon.

CELERY SOUP WITH BLUE CHEESE CREAM

1 head of celery, trimmed, with leaves reserved

4 tbsp butter

1 large onion, peeled and chopped

1 vegetable bouillon cube

2 tbsp all-purpose flour

salt and pepper

1¾ cups (425ml) milk

FOR THE BLUE CHEESE CREAM

1½oz (50g) Danish blue cheese

⅔ cup (150ml) low-fat crème fraîche or light sour cream

saturated fat 13g • unsaturated fat 7g
sodium 866mg • calories 253

1 Chop celery stalks crosswise into ¼in (5mm) thick slices. Melt the butter in a large pan, add the celery and onion, and stir. Cover and cook over low heat for 15 minutes, stirring occasionally.

2 Dissolve the stock cube in 1¾ cups (425ml) boiling water. Sprinkle the flour over the vegetables, stir well, then pour in the stock. Bring to a boil over high heat, stirring all the time. Add salt and pepper, cover, and reduce the heat. Simmer for 10 minutes, or until the celery is very tender.

3 Remove the pan from the heat. Using an electric handheld blender, with the blades below the level of the soup, purée for about 3 minutes, until smooth.

4 Return the soup to medium heat, pour in the milk, and mix well. Bring the soup to a simmer, then check the seasoning. Cover the pan and reduce the heat to low while making the blue cheese cream.

5 Put the blue cheese in a small bowl and mash with a fork until smooth. Add the crème fraîche a little at a time and work into the cheese until evenly combined.

6 Stir the soup one more time, then ladle it into warmed bowls. Place a large spoonful of blue cheese cream in the center of each bowl of soup and swirl it in. Scatter chopped celery leaves on top and serve immediately.

MAKING CROUTONS

Add texture and crunch to soups by garnishing with homemade croutons. For more detailed information, see page 70.

Stack slices of bread and cut into cubes.

Shake with 1–2 tbsp oil in a plastic bag.

Toss over medium heat until golden.

WATERCRESS SOUP

4 tbsp butter

1 large potato (about ¾lb/300g), peeled and roughly chopped

1 large onion, peeled and chopped

1¾ cups (450ml) chicken stock

salt and pepper

½lb (200g) watercress, chopped

2 cups (500ml) milk

1–2 tbsp lemon juice

4 tbsp light cream, to garnish

saturated fat 12g • unsaturated fat 6g
sodium 303mg • calories 314

1 Melt the butter in a large pan. Add the chopped potato and onion and stir well to mix. Cover and cook over low heat for about 15 minutes, stirring occasionally.

2 Pour in the stock and bring to a boil over high heat. Add salt and pepper, cover, and reduce the heat. Simmer for about 10 minutes, or until the potatoes are very tender.

3 Remove the pan from the heat and add the watercress. Using an electric handheld blender, with the blades held below the level of the soup, purée the soup for about 3 minutes, until smooth.

4 Return the soup to medium heat, pour in the milk, and stir well to mix. Bring the soup just to a simmer.

5 Add a little lemon juice, taste the soup, and add more lemon juice if you like. Check the seasoning before serving.

6 Stir the soup one more time, then ladle it into warmed bowls. Spoon 1 tbsp cream in the center of each bowl of soup and swirl it in. Serve immediately.

VARIATION

SPINACH SOUP

Use ½lb (200g) young spinach instead of watercress and remove any tough stems before chopping. Omit the lemon juice and add a few gratings of nutmeg with the salt and pepper in step 2.

CURRIED CARROT SOUP

1 medium onion

3 tbsp sunflower oil

1 tsp Madras (hot) curry powder

2 tsp all-purpose flour

3½ cups (850ml) vegetable stock

1lb (500g) carrots, peeled and sliced

salt and pepper

1–2 tsp lemon juice

FOR THE CILANTRO YOGURT

⅔ cup (150g) plain yogurt

2 tbsp finely chopped fresh cilantro leaves

saturated fat 3g • unsaturated fat 12g
sodium 1072mg • calories 226

1 Peel and chop the onion. Heat the oil in a large pan and cook the onion over medium heat for about 5 minutes, or until softened.

2 Sprinkle the curry powder and flour over the onion, stir well, then pour in the stock and bring to a boil over high heat, stirring all the time.

3 Add the carrots and salt and pepper and bring back to a boil. Reduce the heat, cover, and simmer for 15 minutes, or until the carrots are very tender.

4 Remove the pan from the heat. Using an electric handheld blender, with the blades held below the level of the soup, purée the soup for about 3 minutes, until smooth.

5 Return the soup to medium heat and bring to a simmer. Add a little lemon juice, taste the soup, and add more lemon juice if you like. Check the seasoning.

6 Stir the yogurt and chopped cilantro leaves together in a small bowl until well combined.

7 Stir the soup one more time, then ladle it into warmed bowls. Top each serving with a spoonful of cilantro yogurt and serve immediately.

VARIATION

CURRIED PARSNIP SOUP

Replace the carrots in the main recipe with the same quantity of parsnips. Prepare the parsnips just before using because they have a tendency to discolor once peeled and cut.

EASY TOMATO SOUP

1 vegetable bouillon cube

1 medium onion

2 tbsp butter

2 tbsp all-purpose flour

14oz (400g) canned tomatoes

2 tbsp tomato paste

salt and pepper

1 tsp superfine sugar

saturated fat 3g • unsaturated fat 2g
sodium 648mg
calories 128

1 Dissolve the bouillon cube in 1¾ cups (425ml) boiling water. Peel and chop the onion. Melt the butter in a large pan, add the onion, and stir over low heat for 10 minutes, or until soft.

2 Sprinkle the flour over the onion; stir well. Add the stock, tomatoes (chop if needed), tomato paste, and salt and pepper. Bring to a boil over high heat, stirring all the time, then simmer for 2–3 minutes, stirring occasionally.

3 Place a large sieve over a large bowl, pour the soup into the sieve, and press the solids through with the back of a spoon. Do not use a blender for this soup: it needs to be sieved to remove any tomato cores and seeds.

4 Pour the soup back into the pan, return to medium heat, and bring to a simmer. Add the sugar, then check the seasoning.

VARIATION

TOMATO-PESTO SOUP

Swirl 6–8 tbsp (90–120ml) pesto sauce into the soup before serving. Garnish with basil leaves.

MINESTRONE

2 tbsp olive oil

1 medium onion, peeled and chopped

1 carrot, peeled and chopped

1 celery stalk, trimmed and finely chopped

1 leek, thinly sliced

2 tbsp all-purpose flour

6 cups (1.5 liters) chicken stock

14oz (400g) canned tomatoes

salt and pepper

2oz (50g) dried spaghetti

¼lb (100g) string beans, trimmed and cut into 1in (2.5cm) lengths

¼lb (100g) green cabbage

grated Parmesan cheese, to serve

saturated fat 2g • unsaturated fat 7g
sodium 373mg • calories 243

1 Heat the oil in a large pan. Add the onion, carrot, celery, and leek and cook over low heat for 5 minutes, stirring often, until the vegetables are softened.

2 Sprinkle in the flour and stir to mix. Add the stock, tomatoes (chop if needed), and salt and pepper. Bring to a boil over high heat, stirring constantly. Partially cover, reduce the heat, and simmer for 20 minutes.

3 Break up the spaghetti into short lengths and drop them into the pan. Add the beans. Shred and add the cabbage, stir well, and cook for 10 minutes, or until the vegetables and pasta are tender. Check the seasoning before serving, then sprinkle the soup with grated Parmesan cheese.

CLAM CHOWDER

3 slices bacon, chopped

1 medium onion, peeled and chopped

2 tbsp butter

2 tbsp all-purpose flour

1⅔ cups (400ml) hot milk

1 large potato, peeled and cut into cubes

salt and pepper

⅔ cup (150ml) light cream

¾ cup (100g) corn kernels, defrosted if frozen

10oz (290g) canned baby clams in brine

saturated fat 12g • unsaturated fat 9g
sodium 785mg • calories 374

1 Heat a large pan over low heat for 30 seconds. Then add the bacon and onion and cook for 5 minutes, stirring all the time. Add the butter, stir until melted, then sprinkle in the flour and stir to mix.

2 Remove the pan from the heat and gradually stir in the hot milk. Return the pan to low heat and stir until the mixture thickens and bubbles.

3 Add the potatoes and salt and pepper and cook for 10–15 minutes, or until tender. Add the cream and corn and bring back to a simmer.

4 Drain the clams into a sieve. Add the clams to the soup and heat through gently. Do not allow the soup to boil as this will toughen the clams. Check the seasoning before serving.

MOULES MARINIÈRE

Serve with forks to remove the mussels from their shells, and soup spoons for drinking the liquid.

2 tbsp olive oil

6 scallions, finely chopped

4 celery stalks, trimmed and finely chopped

2 garlic cloves, peeled and crushed

1¼ cups (300ml) dry white wine

1 bouquet garni

4lb (2kg) live mussels, scrubbed (see page 44)

salt and pepper

1¼ cups (300ml) fish stock or water

a large pat of butter

4 tbsp chopped fresh parsley

saturated fat 6g • unsaturated fat 14g
sodium 1582mg • calories 544

1 Heat the oil in a large pan. Add the vegetables and garlic. Cook over medium heat for 5 minutes, or until softened, stirring.

2 Add the wine, bouquet garni, mussels, and salt and pepper. Cover the pan and cook over high heat for about 5 minutes, or until the mussels are open, shaking the pan occasionally.

3 Lift the mussels out into four warmed soup plates, discarding any that are not open. Discard the bouquet garni. Add the stock to the pan and boil for 3–4 minutes, until reduced. Add the butter and whisk until melted, then add the parsley. Check the seasoning and pour the sauce over the mussels.

PASTA

Quick to cook and immensely popular, pasta can be served as a

first course, or as a complete meal with the addition

of a simple salad and some crusty Italian or French bread.

SPAGHETTI WITH TOMATO SAUCE

The sauce can be prepared in advance and kept in the refrigerator for up to 1 week, or in the freezer for up to 3 months.

SERVES 6

1lb (500g) dried spaghetti

leaves from 5 sprigs of fresh basil, shredded

freshly grated Parmesan cheese, to serve

FOR THE TOMATO SAUCE

2 tbsp olive oil

1 large Spanish onion, peeled and finely chopped

14oz (400g) canned chopped tomatoes

2 tsp superfine sugar

1 tsp dried oregano

1 bay leaf

salt and pepper

saturated fat 1g • unsaturated fat 5g
sodium 56mg • calories 373

1 First make the sauce: heat the oil in a medium pan until hot. Add the chopped onion and cook over low heat for about 10 minutes, or until softened but not brown, stirring occasionally.

2 Add the tomatoes, sugar, oregano, bay leaf, and salt and pepper to the pan. Stir well. Bring to a boil over high heat, then reduce the heat to low and simmer gently, uncovered, for about 30 minutes, or until thickened, stirring occasionally.

3 Remove the bay leaf and taste the sauce to check seasoning. Keep hot over low heat while cooking the spaghetti (see below).

4 Drain the spaghetti into a colander, shake well, then return it to the empty pan in which it was cooked, or put it in a warmed large bowl.

5 Pour the tomato sauce over the spaghetti and toss to mix. Serve immediately, sprinkled with the fresh basil. Serve freshly grated Parmesan cheese separately in a small bowl.

VARIATION

TOMATO-CLAM SAUCE

Drain a 10oz (290g) can baby clams in brine. Add the clams to the tomato sauce with the zest and juice of 1 lemon at the end of step 2. Heat through gently. Serve with lemon wedges rather than Parmesan.

COOKING SPAGHETTI

Cooking times vary with different brands, so check the package for precise times. For more detailed information, see page 39.

Bring 4 quarts (4 liters) water to a boil in a large pan. Add 1 tbsp salt.

Coil in the spaghetti, bring back to a boil, and cook for 10–15 minutes.

CANNELLONI BOLOGNESE

*1 quantity Bolognese Sauce
(see Master Recipe, page 82)*

*6oz (175g) cannelloni tubes,
prepared for filling*

a few gratings of nutmeg

salt and pepper

*2½ cups (600ml) medium-
consistency hot white sauce
(see page 68)*

*½ cup (50g) grated
Parmesan cheese*

saturated fat 22g • unsaturated fat 22g
sodium 554mg • calories 839

1 Simmer the Bolognese sauce
in a nonstick pan until no
excess liquid remains, stirring
constantly. Let cool.

2 Preheat the oven to 400°F
(200°C). Grease a baking dish
measuring 8 x 10in (20 x 25cm),
2in (5cm) deep. Spread a little of
the Bolognese sauce in the bottom

3 Use a small plastic bag to fill
the cannelloni tubes: cut a
corner from the sealed end of the
bag to make a ¾in (2cm) opening.
Put 2 large spoonfuls of the
Bolognese sauce into the bag at a
time, and squeeze into each tube.

4 Put the cannelloni tubes close
together in the dish, in a
single layer. Add the nutmeg and
salt and pepper to the white
sauce, then pour the sauce over
the cannelloni, making sure they
are covered. Top with the cheese.

5 Cover with foil and bake for
15 minutes. Remove foil and
bake for 20 minutes, until golden.

PASTA PRIMAVERA

½lb (250g) asparagus tips

*½lb (250g) string beans, trimmed
and cut on the diagonal*

*1 zucchini, trimmed
and cut into sticks*

salt and pepper

5oz (150g) soft goat cheese

*zest and juice of
1 small lemon*

2 tbsp olive oil

*1 large garlic clove, peeled
and crushed*

¾lb (400g) dried penne

saturated fat 5g • unsaturated fat 10g
sodium 189mg • calories 531

1 Plunge the vegetables into a
medium pan of salted boiling
water. Bring back to a boil and
boil for 2 minutes. Drain in a
colander, rinse in cold water, and
shake well. Set aside.

2 Put the cheese in a saucepan
with the lemon zest and juice,
oil, garlic, and salt and pepper.
Stir over low heat until the cheese
has melted. Add the vegetables
and mix well. Set aside.

3 Cook the penne in salted
boiling water for 10 minutes,
or according to package
instructions. Drain, turn into a
large warmed bowl, and add the
vegetable mixture. Toss to mix.

VEGETABLE & NOODLE STIR-FRY

*½lb (250g) dried Chinese
egg noodles*

3 tbsp sunflower oil

*8 scallions, sliced on the
diagonal into short lengths*

*1in (2.5cm) piece of fresh ginger,
peeled and finely chopped*

*3 large garlic cloves, peeled and
very thinly sliced*

*1 large red pepper, cored,
seeded, and diced*

*½lb (225g) small mushrooms,
trimmed and halved*

1 large egg, lightly beaten

dash of Tabasco sauce

salt and pepper

saturated fat 3g • unsaturated fat 14g
sodium 156mg • calories 408

1 Plunge the noodles into a large
pan of boiling water. Remove
from the heat. Stir until noodles
are separated, then cover and let
stand for 4–6 minutes. Drain in a
colander and shake well. Set aside.

2 Heat a wok over high heat for
1–2 minutes until very hot; add
the oil. Heat until it just begins to
smoke, add the scallions and
ginger, and stir-fry for 1 minute.
Add the garlic, red pepper, and
mushrooms. Stir-fry for 2 minutes.

3 Add the noodles and toss to
mix with the vegetables and
heat through. Pour in the beaten
egg, Tabasco, and salt and pepper.
Stir and toss well so the egg coats
the noodles and vegetables. Taste
and add more Tabasco if you like.

STUFFED PASTA SHELLS

Make sure that the filled shells are completely covered in sauce before baking. Any uncovered shells will be chewy and tough.

1 quantity tomato sauce (see page 128)

12 large or 24 medium dried pasta shells

FOR THE FILLING

1lb (500g) frozen leaf spinach, defrosted and well drained

1 cup (250g) mascarpone

2 large eggs, lightly beaten

1 cup (85g) grated Parmesan cheese

1 tbsp shredded fresh basil

a few gratings of nutmeg

salt and pepper

saturated fat 25g • unsaturated fat 19g
sodium 389mg • calories 681

1 Purée the tomato sauce in the pan, using an electric handheld blender with the blades held below the level of the sauce. Alternatively, purée the sauce in a food processor or blender, or work it through a sieve.

2 For the filling, put the spinach and mascarpone in a bowl and beat together with a spoon. Add the eggs, Parmesan, basil, nutmeg, and seasoning. Beat well to mix.

3 Preheat the oven to 400°F (200°C). Grease a baking dish measuring about 8 x 10in (20 x 25cm) and 2in (5cm) deep. Spread a little of the tomato sauce in the bottom of the dish.

4 Cook the pasta shells in salted boiling water for 10–15 minutes, or according to package instructions. Drain in a colander. Fill the pan with cold water. Put the shells back into the pan.

5 Take the shells out of the water one at a time, drain, and fill with the spinach mixture, then pack close together in the dish. Cover them with the remaining tomato sauce. Bake for 35 minutes, or until bubbling.

MEAT LASAGNE

Lasagne that does not need precooking absorbs a lot of liquid during baking, so Bolognese and white sauces should be runny.

1 quantity Bolognese Sauce (see Master Recipe, page 82)

a few gratings of nutmeg

salt and pepper

2½ cups (600ml) medium-consistency hot white sauce (see page 68)

½ cup (50g) Parmesan cheese

about 6 sheets "no precooking required" dried lasagne

saturated fat 22g • unsaturated fat 21g
sodium 550mg • calories 772

1 Preheat the oven to 375°F (190°C). Grease a baking dish measuring about 8 x 10in (20 x 25cm) and 2in (5cm) deep.

2 Spread one third of the Bolognese sauce in the bottom of the dish. Add the nutmeg and salt and pepper to the white sauce, then spread one third over the Bolognese.

3 Grate the Parmesan, then sprinkle one third over the layer of white sauce. Cover with a layer of lasagne sheets, not overlapping them. The dish will probably take 3 sheets, but you may have to break them to fit.

4 Repeat the layers of Bolognese sauce, white sauce, cheese, and lasagne. Finish with layers of the remaining Bolognese, white sauce, and cheese.

5 Bake the lasagne for about 30 minutes, or until bubbling and golden brown.

VARIATION

LOW-FAT LASAGNE

Replace half the white sauce with 1 cup (250g) low-fat cottage cheese, and mix the two together well. Season with 1 heaping tsp Dijon mustard and extra salt and pepper, then use as the white sauce in the main recipe.

VEGETARIAN LASAGNE

1lb (500g) frozen leaf spinach, defrosted and well drained

2½ cups (600ml) medium-consistency hot white sauce (see page 68)

a few gratings of nutmeg

½lb (200g) Emmental cheese, grated

about 6 sheets "no precooking required" dried lasagne

FOR THE MUSHROOM SAUCE

2 tbsp olive oil

1 large onion, peeled and chopped

¾lb (350g) mushrooms, trimmed and sliced

2 large garlic cloves, peeled and crushed

⅓ cup (40g) all-purpose flour

14oz (400g) canned tomatoes

1 tsp sugar

salt and pepper

1 tbsp shredded fresh basil

saturated fat 20g
unsaturated fat 17g
sodium 604mg
calories 668

1 First make the mushroom sauce: heat the oil in a nonstick sauté pan, add the onion, and cook over medium heat for about 5 minutes, or until just beginning to brown. Add the mushrooms and garlic, stir, then cook for about 5 minutes. Sprinkle in the flour and stir well.

2 Add the tomatoes (chop if needed), sugar, and salt and pepper. Bring to a boil, then reduce the heat and simmer, uncovered, for about 15 minutes, or until the sauce has reduced and thickened.

3 Preheat the oven to 375°F (190°C). Grease a baking dish measuring about 8 x 10in (20 x 25cm) and 2in (5cm) deep.

4 Stir the basil into the mushroom sauce. Spread one third in the bottom of the dish.

5 Scatter one third of the spinach over the mushroom sauce, using your fingers. Season the white sauce with nutmeg and salt and pepper, spread one third over the spinach in the dish, then sprinkle with one third of the cheese.

6 Cover with a layer of lasagne sheets, not overlapping them. The dish will probably take 3 sheets, but you may have to break them to fit.

7 Repeat the layers of mushroom sauce, spinach, white sauce, cheese, and lasagne. Finish with mushroom sauce, spinach, white sauce, and cheese. Bake for about 30 minutes, or until golden brown.

GRAINS & LEGUMES

Grains and legumes make nutritious main courses,

or can be used to create tasty and filling accompaniments to

grilled and pan-fried fish, poultry, and meat.

SAFFRON RICE

4 tbsp butter

1 medium onion, peeled and chopped

1 cup (225g) arborio rice

3½ cups (850ml) hot chicken stock

a large pinch of saffron threads

salt and pepper

½ cup (40g) grated Parmesan cheese

saturated fat 11g • unsaturated fat 5g
sodium 416mg • calories 410

1 Melt half the butter in a medium pan. Add the onion and cook over medium heat for 5 minutes, or until softened.

2 Add the rice and stir to coat with butter. Add a ladleful of stock. Stir until absorbed.

3 Add the saffron, salt, and pepper, then a ladleful of stock. Stir until absorbed. If necessary, reduce the heat so the stock is just bubbling.

4 Add the remaining stock a ladleful at a time, stirring constantly, then cook until the rice is creamy and *al dente*. It should take 20–25 minutes. Stir in the remaining butter and Parmesan. Check the seasoning.

DHAL

1½ cups (250g) red or orange lentils

2½ cups (600ml) water

1in (2.5cm) piece of fresh ginger, peeled and grated

1 tsp ground turmeric

1½ tsp salt

1 large garlic clove, peeled

FOR THE TOPPING

2 tbsp sunflower oil

1 tomato, cut into 8 wedges

1 onion, peeled and sliced

½ tsp hot red pepper flakes

fresh cilantro, to garnish

saturated fat 1g • unsaturated fat 7g
sodium 613mg • calories 283

1 Place the lentils, water, ginger, turmeric, and salt in a medium pan. Crush and add the garlic. Bring to a boil, then reduce the heat. Simmer for 20–30 minutes, until soft.

2 Remove pan from the heat and mash the lentils with a potato masher. Add a little hot water if the mixture is too thick. Keep hot.

3 Make the topping: heat the oil in a sauté pan until hot. Add the tomato, onion, and red pepper flakes and stir-fry over medium heat for about 2 minutes.

4 Transfer the dhal to a serving dish, top with the tomato and onion mixture, and garnish with cilantro. Serve immediately.

TABBOULEH

½ cup (100g) bulgur wheat

10 scallions, chopped

1 small bunch of fresh parsley

10 fresh mint sprigs

3 tbsp lemon juice

3 tbsp olive oil

salt and pepper

saturated fat 2g • unsaturated fat 10g
sodium 8mg • calories 203

1 Place the bulgur in a bowl and cover generously with cold water. Let stand for 20–30 minutes. Drain the bulgur into a sieve, squeeze to remove excess water, then place in a bowl.

2 Finely chop the scallions and herbs in a food processor, or by hand with a chef's knife, then add to the bulgur with the lemon juice, oil, and salt and pepper. Stir well, cover, and chill for about 2 hours before serving.

SUMMER COUSCOUS

1 vegetable bouillon cube

1 bunch asparagus, cut
into 1in (2.5cm) lengths

1⅓ cups (250g) couscous

salt and pepper

juice of 1 lemon

3 tbsp olive oil

6 scallions, chopped

¼lb (125g) snow peas, sliced

½ cup (50g) pine nuts, toasted

3 tbsp each chopped fresh
parsley and mint

lemon and mint, to garnish

saturated fat 2g
unsaturated fat 19g
sodium 432mg
calories 374

1 Crumble the bouillon cube into a medium pan. Add 1⅔ cups (400ml) boiling water and stir to dissolve. Bring to a boil, then add the asparagus. Cover the pan and cook for 3 minutes.

2 Place the couscous in a large bowl. Set a colander over the bowl and pour in the stock and asparagus. When the stock has drained, lift off the colander. Add salt and pepper to the couscous and stir well. Cover and let cool.

3 Run cold water over the asparagus to cool it quickly, then dry on paper towels.

4 Add the lemon juice and olive oil to the couscous and toss to mix.

5 Add the asparagus, scallions, snow peas, pine nuts, and chopped herbs. Toss well, then check the seasoning. Serve at room temperature, topped with lemon and mint.

PAN-FRIES

For quick main dishes, pan-fries are perfect – food can be cooked in
a matter of minutes, and go straight from the pan to the table.
For best results, use a good-quality nonstick sauté pan.

GARLIC SHRIMP

16–20 raw jumbo shrimp,
peeled and deveined

5 tbsp (75ml) olive oil

3 garlic cloves, peeled
and crushed

salt and pepper

8oz (250ml) crushed tomatoes

juice of ½ lemon

1 tsp superfine sugar

3 tbsp coarsely chopped
fresh parsley

zest of 1 lemon

*saturated fat 3g • unsaturated fat 16g
sodium 416mg • calories 340*

1 Place the shrimp in a large
bowl with the oil, garlic, and
salt and pepper. Toss well to mix.

2 Heat a large nonstick sauté
pan over high heat for
2 minutes. Add the shrimp with
the oil and garlic and stir for
2 minutes, or until pink. Reduce
the heat to medium and add the
crushed tomatoes, lemon juice,
and sugar. Cook, stirring, for 3–4
minutes. Check seasoning, then
top with parsley and lemon zest.

HERB-CRUSTED FISH

1 cup (75g) fresh white
bread crumbs

2 tbsp chopped mixed fresh
tarragon, dill, and chervil

zest of 1 lemon

4 haddock fillets, each weighing
about ¼lb (125g), skinned

salt and pepper

2 tbsp all-purpose flour

1 large egg, beaten

2 tbsp olive oil

lemon wedges, to serve

*saturated fat 2g • unsaturated fat 8g
sodium 286mg • calories 348*

1 Process the bread crumbs,
herbs, and lemon zest in a food
processor until fine. For a coarser
coating, just mix the ingredients
together in a shallow dish.

2 Prepare each fillet in turn:
sprinkle with salt and pepper,
then coat with the flour and
shake off the excess. Dip each
piece in the beaten egg, then
coat with the crumb mixture.

3 Heat the oil in a large nonstick
sauté pan. Add the fish and
cook over medium heat for
3 minutes on each side, or until
golden brown and crisp. Serve hot,
with lemon wedges for squeezing.

TURKEY SEVILLE

4 turkey breast cutlets

salt and pepper

2 tbsp olive oil

12 large fresh sage leaves

2 tbsp butter

4 tbsp sherry

⅔ cup (150ml) heavy cream

*saturated fat 17g • unsaturated fat 18g
sodium 126mg • calories 492*

1 Pound the turkey breast
cutlets, then cut each one into
three pieces. Sprinkle each piece
with salt and pepper.

2 Heat the oil in a large nonstick
sauté pan. Add the sage and
cook over high heat until crisp.
Remove from pan and set aside.

3 Melt the butter in the pan
until foaming. Add the turkey
and pan-fry over high heat for
2 minutes on each side, or until
tender. Lift out into a serving dish
and keep hot. Add the sherry and
cream to the pan and bring to a
boil, stirring. Check the
seasoning, pour over the turkey,
and top with the sage leaves.

CAJUN-STYLE CHICKEN

2 tsp dried oregano

2 tsp sweet paprika

½ tsp ground ginger

½ tsp black pepper

¼ tsp cayenne

1 tbsp olive oil

4 skinless boneless chicken breasts

salt

a few sprigs of thyme, to garnish

saturated fat 2g • unsaturated fat 5g
sodium 80mg • calories 173

1 Combine the oregano, spices, and oil in a bowl, then rub over the chicken breasts to coat.

2 Heat a large nonstick sauté pan over high heat for 2 minutes. Add the chicken, smooth side down. Pan-fry for 2–3 minutes, until just beginning to blacken.

3 Turn the chicken over, reduce the heat, and cook for 3–6 minutes, until the juices run clear. Sprinkle with a little salt and the thyme just before serving.

VARIATION

CAJUN-STYLE SEA BASS

Substitute 4 thick steaks of sea bass, skinned, for the chicken. Coat with the same spicy mixture as for the chicken and pan-fry for 3 minutes on each side. Check to see whether the fish looks opaque all along the cut edge. If not, cook for a few seconds longer.

STIR-FRIES

Colorful and fresh-tasting, stir-fries are healthy and quick. A wok is

the traditional pan for cooking, but if you haven't got one, a large

nonstick sauté pan can be used – the deeper the sides the better.

SPICED SCALLOPS & SHRIMP

1 tbsp sunflower oil

2 large carrots, peeled and cut into thin sticks

¾lb (400g) large shrimp in shells, peeled and deveined

½lb (250g) bay scallops

6–8 scallions, sliced

1 cup (250ml) coconut milk

1 tsp superfine sugar

salt

fresh cilantro leaves, to garnish

FOR THE SPICE MIX

3 garlic cloves, peeled

1in (2.5cm) piece of fresh ginger, peeled

2 tsp mild curry powder

2 tbsp sunflower oil

saturated fat 9g • unsaturated fat 12g sodium 312mg • calories 368

1 First make the spice mix: put all the ingredients in a food processor fitted with the metal blade and process until smooth, or pound in a mortar and pestle.

2 Heat a wok over high heat for 1–2 minutes until very hot. Add the oil and heat until it just begins to smoke.

3 Reduce the heat to medium, add the carrots, and stir-fry for 1 minute. Add the spice mix and stir-fry for 2 minutes. Add the shrimp, scallops, and scallions. Stir-fry over high heat for about 3 minutes, until shrimp are pink.

4 Add the coconut milk, sugar, and salt. Stir and heat until bubbling. Garnish with cilantro.

VEGETABLES WITH MARINATED TOFU

1lb (500g) firm tofu

2 garlic cloves, peeled and finely chopped

2 tbsp finely chopped fresh thyme

1 tbsp sesame oil

salt and pepper

1 vegetable bouillon cube

2 tbsp sunflower oil

2 medium onions, peeled and thinly sliced

½lb (250g) mushrooms, trimmed and thinly sliced

¾lb (300g) cauliflower florets

¾lb (300g) broccoli florets

⅔ cup (150ml) dry white wine

1 tbsp cornstarch

saturated fat 3g • unsaturated fat 15g sodium 447mg • calories 319

1 Drain and cube the tofu and place in a dish. Sprinkle the garlic, thyme, sesame oil, and salt and pepper over the tofu. Cover and marinate for 20 minutes.

2 Dissolve the bouillon cube in ⅔ cup (150ml) boiling water. Heat a wok over high heat for 1–2 minutes until very hot. Add the tofu and marinade and stir-fry over medium heat until lightly browned. Transfer to a plate.

3 Heat the sunflower oil in the wok, add the onions, and stir-fry for 3–4 minutes. Add the mushrooms, stir-fry for 2 minutes, then add the cauliflower and broccoli and stir-fry for 2 minutes. Pour in the wine and stock.

4 Blend the cornstarch with 2 tbsp water, then add water to measure ⅓ cup (100ml). Pour into the wok, bring to a boil, and stir-fry until the vegetables are tender. Add salt and pepper, then sprinkle the tofu over the top.

VARIATION

VEGETABLES WITH MARINATED STEAK

Substitute 2 fillet steaks (total weight about ¾lb/350g) for the tofu and a beef bouillon cube for the vegetable bouillon cube. Cut the steaks into thin strips across the grain. Stir-fry for 2–3 minutes.

HOISIN PORK

2 medium carrots

8oz (200g) canned baby corn

4–6 scallions

8 thin slices of lemon

3 tbsp sunflower oil

¾lb (400g) pork cutlet, pounded and sliced into thin strips

1 garlic clove, peeled and crushed

5 tbsp hoisin sauce

2 tbsp dry sherry

¼lb (100g) fresh bean sprouts

fresh cilantro, to garnish

saturated fat 4g
unsaturated fat 15g
sodium 1168mg
calories 348

1 Peel the carrots and cut into thin sticks. Cut the corn into 1½in (4cm) lengths. Slice the scallions on the diagonal. Cut the lemon slices into quarters.

2 Heat a wok over high heat for 1–2 minutes until very hot. Add 2 tbsp of the oil and heat until it just begins to smoke. Add the carrots, corn, scallions, and lemon and stir-fry over medium heat for 2 minutes, or until the corn is tender.

3 Remove the vegetables with a slotted spoon. Add half the pork and stir-fry for 3 minutes. Remove with the slotted spoon. Heat the remaining oil in the wok, add the remaining pork and the garlic, and stir-fry for 3 minutes.

4 Return the vegetables and pork to the wok, add the hoisin sauce and sherry, and stir-fry until bubbling. Add the bean sprouts and toss to mix. Serve hot, garnished with cilantro.

STOVETOP GRILLS

A ridged cast-iron pan like the one shown here is essential for stovetop grilling. It will enable you to cook quickly in the minimum amount of fat, and the food will be charred with attractive stripes.

VEGETABLES WITH SALSA VERDE

1 small eggplant

2 medium zucchini

4 medium peppers (2 red, 2 yellow)

1 large Spanish onion

1 tbsp olive oil

2 tsp balsamic vinegar

Parmesan cheese, to garnish

FOR THE SALSA VERDE

1 medium onion, peeled and finely chopped

2 tbsp chopped fresh parsley

2 tbsp shredded fresh basil

6½ tbsp (100ml) olive oil

2 tbsp drained capers, finely chopped

salt and pepper

saturated fat 4g • unsaturated fat 29g
sodium 66mg • calories 370

1 First make the salsa verde: place the onion, herbs, olive oil, capers, and salt and pepper in a large bowl and mix together until well combined, then taste to check the seasoning. Cover the bowl with plastic wrap and place in the refrigerator to chill the salsa while preparing and cooking the vegetables.

2 Trim the ends off the eggplant. Cut lengthwise in half, then cut each half crosswise into ½in (1cm) slices and place in a bowl.

3 Trim the zucchini and cut into ½in (1cm) slices on the diagonal. Add to the bowl of eggplant slices.

4 Halve, core, and seed the peppers, then cut each half lengthwise into three wide strips. Trim away any white ribs so the strips will lie flat. Add to the bowl.

5 Peel the onion and cut it lengthwise into eight wedges. Add to the bowl, sprinkle in the olive oil and salt and pepper, and toss well to mix all the ingredients together.

6 Preheat a stovetop grill over high heat for about 10 minutes. Reduce the heat to medium, then place the vegetables on the pan in batches, in a single layer. Cook for about 2 minutes on each side, until they are lightly charred but still crisp. As each batch is cooked, transfer to a large bowl.

7 When all the vegetables are in the bowl, sprinkle with the balsamic vinegar and mix well. Arrange the vegetables on a large serving platter, spoon over the salsa, and shave Parmesan cheese over the top. Serve warm or cold.

FRUITY PORK CHOPS

4 pork loin chops, excess fat removed

1 tbsp olive oil

salt and pepper

FOR THE FRESH FRUIT SALSA

¼ cup (75g) raisins

1 crisp apple, finely chopped

1 orange, peeled and finely chopped

2 tbsp white or brown sugar

1 tbsp white wine vinegar

2 tbsp chopped fresh mint

saturated fat 3g • unsaturated fat 7g
sodium 91mg • calories 286

1 First make the salsa: soak the raisins in boiling water for 10 minutes, drain, and mix with the remaining ingredients. Chill.

2 Brush the chops with oil. Preheat a stovetop grill over high heat for about 10 minutes. Reduce the heat to medium, place the chops on the pan, and cook for 5 minutes on each side, or until the juices run clear when the meat is cut. Season and serve with the salsa.

STEAK WITH ONION MARMELADE

The French term *marmelade* is used to describe fruit or vegetables that are cooked slowly until they are very soft. If you are serving wine with the meal, add a dash to the marmelade.

4 rump or sirloin steaks about ¼lb (125g) each, fat snipped

1 tbsp olive oil

ONION MARMELADE

2 tbsp olive oil

3 large Spanish onions (1½lb/700g), peeled and thinly sliced

1 tbsp chopped fresh thyme

salt and pepper

saturated fat 7g • unsaturated fat 17g
sodium 89mg • calories 409

1 First make the marmelade: heat the oil in a nonstick sauté pan, add the onions, and cook over medium heat for 10 minutes, or until softened but not browned, stirring often.

2 Turn the heat down to low and cover the pan. Continue to cook for 5–10 minutes, or until the onions are very soft and pale golden, stirring from time to time. Add the thyme and salt and pepper, stir, re-cover, and remove from the heat.

3 Preheat a stovetop grill over high heat for about 10 minutes.

4 Return the marmelade to the heat. Brush the steaks with olive oil. Reduce the heat to medium and place the steaks on the pan. Cook for 2 minutes, then turn the steaks over and cook for 3 minutes on the other side, or until cooked to your liking (cut into one steak to see how the cooking is progressing).

5 Just before serving, sprinkle the steaks with salt and pepper and top with the onions.

BROILED DISHES

Broiling preserves the natural flavor of food, and is one of the fastest and easiest of cooking methods. No special equipment is required, but no two broilers are the same, so cooking times are approximate.

TANDOORI CHICKEN

4 skinless, boneless chicken breasts

FOR THE TANDOORI MARINADE

3 tbsp plain yogurt

3 tbsp sunflower oil

2 tbsp cold water

1 small onion, peeled and grated

1 garlic clove, peeled and crushed

2 tsp ground ginger

1 tsp ground turmeric

1 tsp Madras (hot) curry powder

*saturated fat 2g • unsaturated fat 6g
sodium 110mg • calories 195*

1 Mix all the marinade ingredients together in a large bowl. Add the chicken breasts and turn to coat in the marinade. Cover the bowl with plastic wrap and marinate in the refrigerator for 8–24 hours.

2 Line the broiler pan with foil. Preheat the broiler on high for about 5 minutes before cooking.

3 Drain the chicken breasts and arrange them on the rack of the broiler pan. Reduce the heat to medium-high. Broil the chicken, about 4in (10cm) from the heat, for about 6 minutes on each side, or until the juices are clear when the chicken is cut.

BROILED TROUT

½ cucumber, peeled

3 tbsp butter

2 tbsp chopped fresh dill

juice of 1 lemon

salt and pepper

*4 trout, each weighing about
¾lb (375g), boned*

*saturated fat 7g • unsaturated fat 9g
sodium 221mg • calories 385*

1 Cut the cucumber lengthwise in half, scoop out the seeds with a spoon, then slice crosswise.

2 Melt half the butter in a saucepan. Add the cucumber, toss over low heat for 2 minutes, then remove from the heat and add the dill, lemon juice, and salt and pepper. Stir to mix, then spread the cucumber out in a foil-lined broiler pan. Preheat the broiler 5 minutes before cooking.

3 Season the trout inside and out, then spread the remaining butter over the skin. Broil, about 4in (10cm) from the heat, for 4–7 minutes on each side, until the flesh flakes easily when tested with a fork. Serve with the cucumber.

HAMBURGERS

Quantities given here are for two large burgers. If you prefer, shape the mixture into four smaller burgers. Serve in buns with a side salad.

SERVES 2

1lb (500g) ground beef

1 small onion, peeled and grated (optional)

salt and pepper

1–2 tbsp sunflower oil

*saturated fat 10g • unsaturated fat 18g
sodium 166mg • calories 454*

1 Place the meat in a bowl and add the onion, if using. Add salt and pepper and mix lightly.

2 Form the mixture into two large burgers, using wet hands to keep the mixture from sticking.

3 Line the broiler pan with foil and preheat the broiler for about 5 minutes before cooking.

4 Brush the burgers with oil on one side. Lay them, oiled side down, on the rack of the broiler pan and brush the top of each burger with oil. Broil, about 4in (10cm) from the heat, for 2–3 minutes on each side for rare burgers, 4–5 minutes for medium, 6 minutes for well done.

SEAFOOD KEBABS

¾lb (350g) firm white fish fillet, such as monkfish, skinned

¾lb (350g) salmon fillet (thick end), skinned

8 jumbo shrimp in shells, peeled and deveined

6 baby zucchini, trimmed and each cut into 4 pieces

16 cherry tomatoes

FOR THE MARINADE

6 tbsp (90ml) olive oil

1 tbsp balsamic vinegar

3 tbsp chopped fresh tarragon or basil

2 large garlic cloves, peeled and crushed

salt and pepper

*saturated fat 3g • unsaturated fat 15g
sodium 183mg • calories 341*

1 First make the marinade: put all the ingredients in a large bowl and stir well to mix.

2 Cut the white fish and salmon into 16 equal-size chunks. Place in the marinade, add the shrimp, and mix. Cover and refrigerate for up to 6 hours.

3 Line the broiler pan with foil. Just before cooking, preheat the broiler for 5 minutes on high.

4 Lift the fish and shrimp out of the marinade (reserve the marinade). Thread 2 chunks of each type of fish, 1 shrimp, 3 pieces of zucchini, and 2 tomatoes onto each of eight skewers.

5 Arrange the skewers on the rack of the broiler pan and brush with the marinade. Reduce the heat to medium-high. Broil the kebabs, about 4in (10cm) from the heat, for about 10 minutes, turning them twice and brushing with the marinade. Check that the fish is opaque in the center.

6 Serve the fish and vegetables on the skewers on a large platter, or slide them off and serve them on individual plates.

CASSEROLES

These casseroles are all made in a single pot. Once they are simmering, they can be left unattended. You can prepare them the day before and the flavors will improve, but reheat thoroughly (see page 62).

CHICKEN CACCIATORE

The Italian word *cacciatore* means "hunter's style." Dishes with this name are usually rustic and homely, and often contain mushrooms. If you prefer, you can use 8 chicken thighs instead of 4 chicken legs.

2 tbsp olive oil

4 whole chicken legs, skinned

1 large onion, peeled and roughly chopped

2 green peppers, cored, seeded, and sliced

1 garlic clove, peeled and crushed

⅓ cup (40g) all-purpose flour

⅔ cup (200ml) red wine

1½ cups (400g) canned chopped tomatoes

½ tsp granulated sugar

½ tsp dried oregano

salt and pepper

¼lb (140g) mushrooms, trimmed and cut lengthwise into quarters

chopped fresh parsley, to garnish

saturated fat 2g • unsaturated fat 8g sodium 98mg • calories 257

1 Preheat the oven to 325°F (160°C). Heat the oil in a medium pot over medium heat. Add the chicken pieces and cook, turning them over occasionally with tongs, for about 10 minutes, or until they are browned on all sides. Lift out the chicken and set aside on a plate.

2 Add the onion, peppers, and garlic to the pot and cook for about 10 minutes, or until softened, stirring occasionally.

3 Sprinkle the flour over the vegetables and stir for a few moments. Pour in the red wine, stir well, and bring to a boil. Add the tomatoes with their juice, the sugar, oregano, and salt and pepper. Bring back to a boil, stirring.

4 Return the chicken pieces to the pot and bring back to a boil, stirring, then cover and transfer to the oven. Cook for about 40 minutes, adding the mushrooms for the last 5 minutes. Stir the mushrooms into the sauce so they are covered.

5 Pierce the chicken with the tip of a knife to see if the juices run clear and the meat is tender, then check the seasoning of the sauce. Sprinkle liberally with chopped parsley just before serving.

VEGETABLE CURRY

1½lb (750g) vegetables (such as cauliflower, potatoes, carrots, green beans), peeled/trimmed

3 tbsp sunflower oil

2 medium onions, peeled and chopped

1 large garlic clove, peeled and crushed

1in (2.5cm) piece of fresh ginger, peeled and finely chopped

1 tbsp garam masala

14oz (400g) canned chopped tomatoes

¾ cup (175ml) pineapple juice

salt

saturated fat 2g • unsaturated fat 11g sodium 64mg • calories 247

1 Cut the vegetables into similar-size pieces so they cook evenly.

2 Heat the oil in a medium pan. Add the onions and cook over medium heat for 10 minutes, or until browned, stirring often.

3 Add the garlic, ginger, garam masala, tomatoes, pineapple juice, and salt and bring to a simmer, stirring. Add all of the vegetables, cover, and cook over low heat for 15 minutes, or until just tender. Check the seasoning.

MOROCCAN-STYLE SPICED LAMB

This casserole uses shoulder of lamb, which is well marbled with fat and has a very good flavor. If you like, prepare the dish a day ahead, cool, then chill in the refrigerator overnight. The next day, remove all the fat that has solidified on the surface, then reheat the casserole until bubbling before serving.

2 tbsp sunflower oil

1 large onion, peeled and finely chopped

1½–2lb (750g–1kg) boneless shoulder of lamb, trimmed and cut into 1½in (4cm) cubes

½ tsp ground allspice

½ tsp ground ginger

2 tbsp all-purpose flour

salt and pepper

16oz (500g) boxed or canned crushed tomatoes

¾ cup (175g) dried apricots, halved

3in (7.5cm) piece of cinnamon stick, broken crosswise in half

saffron rice (see page 132), to serve

1 tbsp sesame seeds

*saturated fat 21g • unsaturated fat 28g
sodium 291mg • calories 760*

1 Heat the oil in a medium pot. Add the onion and cook over medium heat for 10 minutes, or until golden, stirring occasionally.

2 Add the cubes of lamb to the pot, then sprinkle in the spices, flour, and salt and pepper. Cook, stirring and turning the lamb, for 5 minutes, or until the meat has lost its redness.

3 Pour the tomatoes into a measuring cup and add enough cold water to make 2½ cups (600ml). Pour onto the lamb, stirring. Add the apricots and cinnamon; heat until a few bubbles appear. Cover and cook over low heat for 45 minutes.

4 Check from time to time to make sure the liquid is simmering very gently, with just the occasional bubble.

5 Uncover the pot and cook for 15 minutes longer, or until the meat is tender enough to cut with the side of a fork. The cooking liquid should be thick enough to just coat the meat. Check the seasoning.

6 Spoon the stew onto a bed of saffron rice, removing the pieces of cinnamon as you come across them. Sprinkle with the sesame seeds just before serving.

ROASTS

A roast is ideal for a special occasion, especially when you

can spare more time for preparation and cooking. Turn the

page to find accompaniments to serve with your chosen roast.

ROAST TURKEY WITH CHESTNUT STUFFING

If you can't get fresh chestnuts, use ¼lb (120g) dried chestnuts and soak them overnight in cold water.

SERVES 8–10

8–10lb (4–5kg) turkey, defrosted if frozen

3 tbsp butter, at room temperature

FOR THE CHESTNUT STUFFING

6 bacon slices, diced

½lb (250g) fresh chestnuts, cooked, peeled, and chopped

1 cup (50g) fresh white bread crumbs

1 medium egg, beaten

½ bunch of watercress, trimmed and finely chopped

salt and pepper

saturated fat 8g • unsaturated fat 10g
sodium 446mg • calories 460

1 First make the stuffing: put the bacon in a nonstick sauté pan and cook over low heat until the fat is released. Add the chestnuts and cook over medium heat for 10 minutes, or until the bacon is crisp. Add the bread crumbs.

2 Transfer to a bowl and let cool. Add the egg, watercress, and salt and pepper and mix well.

3 Preheat oven to 350°F (180°C). Spoon the cold stuffing into the neck end of the bird, pull the skin over, and secure with a skewer. Twist the wing tips up and over; tie wings and legs with string.

4 Spread the butter over the bird, sprinkle with salt and pepper, then place, breast side up, on a rack in a roasting pan. If you have a meat thermometer, push it into the thickest part of a thigh, away from the bone.

5 Roast for 3–3½ hours, until the juices run clear when a skewer is inserted into the thigh. If using a thermometer, the temperature should read 185°F (85°C). If the bird browns before it is cooked, cover with foil and continue roasting. Let the bird stand, wrapped in foil, while you make the gravy (see page 103).

BEEF WELLINGTON

1½lb (750g) piece of thick end of beef tenderloin

2 tbsp butter, at room temperature

pepper

¾lb (350g) frozen puff pastry, defrosted

1 large egg, beaten

saturated fat 17g • unsaturated fat 24g
sodium 416mg • calories 681

1 Preheat oven to 425°F (220°C). Trim any fat or sinew from the beef. Place the meat in a small roasting pan, spread the butter over the meat, and sprinkle with pepper. Roast for 20 minutes for rare beef, 30 minutes for medium. Remove from the oven. Let cool.

2 Roll out the pastry on a lightly floured surface to a rectangle three times wider than the beef and about 8in (20cm) longer.

3 Place the beef in the middle of the pastry. Bring the two long sides up over the beef to meet in the middle with a 1in (2.5cm) overlap. Brush the underside of the overlap with beaten egg and press to seal. Place the bundle seam side down on a baking sheet, trim the ends of the pastry, leaving enough to fold underneath, and tuck edges under.

4 Brush the pastry with beaten egg. Roll the pastry trimmings into a long strip. Cut into thin strips and arrange in a crisscross pattern on top of the parcel. The beef can be baked at this stage, or wrapped in plastic wrap and refrigerated for up to 12 hours.

5 Preheat the oven to the same temperature as before. Brush pastry with beaten egg again and bake for 30 minutes. If the pastry browns too quickly, cover with foil. Serve cut into thick slices.

RACK OF LAMB WITH HERB CRUST

SERVES 4–6

1 large egg, beaten

2 racks of lamb, prepared and chined by the butcher, excess fat removed

¾ cup (40g) fresh bread crumbs

2 tbsp each finely chopped fresh parsley and mint

2 scallions, finely chopped

1 garlic clove, peeled and crushed

zest of 1 lemon

salt and pepper

saturated fat 11g
unsaturated fat 11g
sodium 197mg
calories 385

1 Preheat the oven to 400°F (200°C). Brush beaten egg over the fat on one side of each rack of lamb.

2 Combine the bread crumbs, herbs, scallions, garlic, and lemon zest in a bowl. Add salt and pepper and 1 tbsp of the remaining beaten egg and mix together to form a wet paste.

3 Divide the paste in half and spread one portion over the fat side of each rack.

4 Place the racks, herb crust up, in a roasting pan, with the bones pointing toward the center. Roast for 40–50 minutes for medium-rare (pink) meat, 1 hour for medium.

5 Remove from the oven, cover with foil, and let stand in a warm place for 10 minutes before slicing into individual chops. If you like, serve with onion gravy (see pages 86–87).

VEGETABLES

For a special occasion, serve one or two of these accompaniments

with roast meat or poultry. For boiled, mashed, and roast

potatoes, see pages 60–61; for plain cooked vegetables, see page 161.

SAVOY CABBAGE STIR-FRY

If you prefer, use a heaping tablespoon of coarse-grain mustard instead of soy sauce.

2 tbsp olive oil

1 large onion, peeled and thinly sliced

2 garlic cloves, peeled and crushed

1 small Savoy cabbage, cored and finely shredded

2 tbsp light soy sauce

saturated fat 1g • unsaturated fat 7g sodium 542mg • calories 123

1 Heat a wok or a large sauté pan over high heat for 1–2 minutes, until very hot. Add 1 tbsp of the oil and heat until it just begins to smoke. Reduce the heat to medium, add the onion and garlic, and stir-fry for about 2 minutes.

2 Add the remaining 1 tbsp oil to the wok, and then add the cabbage. Stir-fry for 2 minutes, then sprinkle the soy sauce over the vegetables and toss to mix.

PAN-FRIED CAULIFLOWER & BROCCOLI

The cauliflower and broccoli can be parboiled in advance – after draining in the colander, rinse with cold water, then pan-fry them just before serving.

¾lb (350g) cauliflower florets

¾lb (350g) broccoli florets

salt and pepper

3 tbsp olive oil

1 tbsp balsamic vinegar

saturated fat 2g • unsaturated fat 10g sodium 16mg • calories 160

1 Trim the cauliflower and broccoli florets, then cut lengthwise in half.

2 Bring a medium pan of water to a boil. Add salt, then the cauliflower and broccoli florets, and cook for about 3 minutes, or until tender but still firm. Drain well in a colander.

3 Heat the oil in a large nonstick sauté pan over medium heat. Add the cauliflower and broccoli and cook, stirring and tossing, for 2 minutes, or until the vegetables are hot. Sprinkle with pepper and drizzle over the balsamic vinegar.

BAKED FENNEL

6 small fennel bulbs

salt and pepper

1 tbsp olive oil

½ cup (40g) grated Parmesan cheese

saturated fat 3g • unsaturated fat 4g sodium 126mg • calories 97

1 Preheat the oven to 425°F (220°C). Trim off the tops and ends of the fennel, leaving enough base for the bulbs to hold together. Cut each one lengthwise in half.

2 Bring a medium pan of water to a boil. Add salt, then the fennel, and cook for 10–15 minutes, or until almost tender. Drain well in a colander.

3 Place the fennel in a baking dish. Sprinkle with the oil and salt and pepper and turn to coat. Spread the fennel halves out, cut sides up, in the dish.

4 Sprinkle the Parmesan over the fennel. Bake for about 20 minutes, or until the fennel is tender when tested with a skewer and the topping is golden brown.

GARLIC CREAM POTATOES

For a lighter version, replace the heavy cream with crème fraîche.

SERVES 4–6

1¾lb (900g) potatoes, peeled

salt and pepper

1¼ cups (300ml) heavy cream

2 large garlic cloves, peeled and crushed

saturated fat 27g • unsaturated fat 15g sodium 100mg • calories 561

1 Preheat the oven to 400°F (200°C). Generously butter a baking dish measuring about 8 x 10in (20 x 25cm) and 2in (5cm) deep.

2 Cut the potatoes into slices about ¼in (3mm) thick. Layer half the slices in the dish and sprinkle with salt and pepper. Pour the cream into a cup, then add the crushed garlic and mix well. Pour half this mixture evenly over the potatoes in the dish.

3 Cover with the remaining potato slices, layering them evenly. Sprinkle with salt and pepper, then pour over the rest of the garlic cream.

4 Cover the dish with buttered foil and bake for 30 minutes. Remove the foil and bake for about 50 minutes, or until the potatoes are tender when pierced and the top is brown.

RATATOUILLE

If you like crunchy vegetables, reduce the cooking time by about half, and add the zucchini for the last 10 minutes only so that they retain their fresh green color and firm texture.

4 tbsp olive oil

1 large Spanish onion, peeled and sliced

1 large eggplant, sliced into rounds about ½in (1cm) thick

4 small zucchini, about ½lb (300g), trimmed and sliced

6 tomatoes, peeled, halved, and seeded

1 large red pepper, cored, seeded, and sliced

1 large garlic clove, peeled and crushed

1 tsp granulated sugar

salt and pepper

1 tbsp shredded fresh basil

saturated fat 2g • unsaturated fat 14g sodium 13mg • calories 213

1 Heat the oil in a large nonstick skillet. Add the onion and cook over medium heat for about 10 minutes, or until softened, stirring often.

2 Add the remaining vegetables, the garlic, sugar, and salt and pepper. Stir well. Cover the pan and cook over low heat for about 45 minutes, or until the vegetables are tender but still retain their shape. Stir gently from time to time. At the end of cooking, check the seasoning and sprinkle with the shredded basil.

SWEET & SOUR RED CABBAGE

Cooked this way, red cabbage will lose its bright color and become a more mellow reddish brown. It reheats very successfully, and can be made up to 2 days ahead.

1¾lb (900g) hard red cabbage, cored and coarsely shredded

1lb (450g) apples, quartered, cored, peeled, and sliced

½lb (250g) onions, peeled and finely chopped

3 tbsp wine vinegar

3 tbsp light brown sugar

¼ tsp ground cinnamon

1 large garlic clove, peeled and crushed

salt and pepper

saturated fat 0g • unsaturated fat 1g sodium 25mg • calories 153

1 Preheat the oven to 300°F (150°C). Combine all the ingredients together in a large ovenproof pan and bring to a boil, stirring well.

2 Cover and transfer to the oven. Cook for 2–2½ hours, or until the cabbage is very tender, stirring once or twice. Once the cabbage is cooked, serve it immediately, or turn the oven off and leave the pan inside – the cabbage will retain its heat for up to 20 minutes.

SALADS

Packages of washed leaves from the supermarket are a

handy timesaver for the busy cook, but can become monotonous.

The following recipes will add interest to your salad repertoire.

MIXED GREEN SALAD

SERVES 4–6

4–6 scallions, trimmed and sliced

6 celery stalks, trimmed and cut into very thin diagonal slices

1 small fennel bulb, trimmed and thinly sliced

4–6 tbsp French dressing (see page 69)

½ cucumber

6oz (200g) package mixed salad leaves

1 Boston lettuce

about 20 leaves of arugula, baby spinach, or mâche

salt and pepper

*saturated fat 2g • unsaturated fat 11g
sodium 109mg • calories 148*

1 Mix the scallions, celery, and fennel in a large salad bowl. Add the dressing and toss well.

2 Cut the cucumber lengthwise in half, then cut across into thick slices. Tear all the leaves into manageable-size pieces.

3 Place half the cucumber and half the leaves in the bowl. Add salt and pepper, then the remaining cucumber and leaves. Season again. Cover and chill for up to 4 hours. Toss before serving.

COLESLAW

½ green cabbage, about ¾lb (325g)

4–6 tbsp French dressing (see page 69)

½ small onion, peeled and finely chopped

1 tsp Dijon mustard

salt and pepper

3 celery stalks

2 carrots

4–5 tbsp mayonnaise

*saturated fat 4g • unsaturated fat 26g
sodium 125mg • calories 324*

1 Cut the cabbage lengthwise into quarters, then remove the core from each piece. Shred the cabbage, either with a chef's knife or in a food processor fitted with the slicing disk.

2 Place the cabbage in a large bowl and add the dressing, onion, mustard, and salt and pepper. Toss to mix. Cover tightly and chill for about 8 hours.

3 Trim the celery and thinly slice on the diagonal. Peel the carrots, then grate them coarsely on a box grater or in a food processor fitted with the coarse-grating disk. Add to the cabbage, toss to mix, then add the mayonnaise and stir to combine. Cover tightly and chill for 1 hour. Check seasoning before serving.

SALAD DRESSINGS

Homemade dressings taste better than store-bought ones. For quantities of ingredients and further information, see page 69.

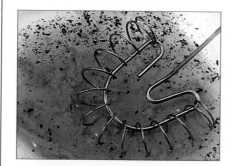

For French dressing, whisk wine vinegar, olive oil, and seasonings by hand.

For mayonnaise, work egg, sunflower oil, and seasonings in a food processor.

POTATO, APPLE & CELERY SALAD

1½lb (750g) new potatoes

salt and pepper

½ cup (120ml) French dressing
(see page 69)

2 crisp apples

juice of 1 lemon

4 celery stalks, trimmed and cut
into slices ¼in (5mm) thick

3 scallions, trimmed
and shredded

4 tbsp mayonnaise

chopped fresh parsley, to garnish

*saturated fat 5g • unsaturated fat 30g
sodium 102mg • calories 480*

1 Scrub the potatoes and cook in
a pan of salted boiling water for
15–20 minutes, until tender.

2 Drain the potatoes, leave them
until cool enough to handle,
then cut in half. Place them in a
large bowl and sprinkle the
dressing over them. Let cool.

3 Quarter, core, and dice the
unpeeled apples and place
them in a bowl. Pour the lemon
juice over the top and toss to
mix. This prevents discoloration.

4 Add the apples to the cold
potatoes with the celery,
scallions, and mayonnaise. Toss
well to mix. Check the seasoning
and sprinkle the salad with
parsley before serving.

FOUR-BEAN SALAD

SERVES 6–8

14oz (420g) canned chickpeas

14oz (420g) canned cannellini

14oz (420g) canned red beans

14oz (420g) canned
black eye peas

6 tbsp (90ml) French dressing
(see page 69)

1 large garlic clove, peeled
and crushed

4 celery stalks, trimmed and
cut into slices ¼in (5mm) wide

1 medium red onion, peeled
and chopped

salt and pepper

*saturated fat 3g • unsaturated fat 19g
sodium 1402mg • calories 458*

1 Drain all the beans in a
colander, then rinse under cold
running water. Drain well. Line a
baking sheet with a double layer of
paper towels. Spread the beans on
the paper and shake the tray until
the beans are no longer wet.

2 Pour the dressing into a large
bowl, add the beans, garlic,
celery, onion, and salt and pepper
and toss well. Cover and chill for
4 hours. Taste to check the
seasoning before serving.

VARIATION

BEAN SALAD WITH TUNA

Drain 7oz (200g) canned tuna in
oil; break into large chunks. Fold
into the bean salad before chilling.
Garnish with 3 hard-boiled eggs,
shelled, cooled, and quartered.

CAESAR SALAD

A classic Caesar salad includes
a raw or coddled egg, but
here mayonnaise is used instead.

4 Romaine lettuces,
leaves separated

1 bunch arugula, leaves only

2oz (50g) canned anchovies
in oil, drained (optional)

croutons made from 4 slices
of white bread

2oz (50g) Parmesan cheese,
grated or in shavings

FOR THE DRESSING

3 tbsp mayonnaise

juice of ½ lemon

2 tsp Worcestershire sauce

1 garlic clove, peeled and crushed

1 tbsp olive oil

salt and pepper

*saturated fat 8g • unsaturated fat 32g
sodium 825mg • calories 510*

1 First make the dressing: put the
ingredients in a small bowl and
whisk to mix. Check seasoning.

2 Tear the lettuce and arugula
leaves into a large bowl. If
using anchovies, snip them into
small pieces over the bowl, using
scissors. Add the croutons and
Parmesan cheese.

3 Pour the dressing over the
salad, toss well to mix, and
serve immediately.

NIÇOISE SALAD

*½lb (250g) new
potatoes, scrubbed*

salt and pepper

*½lb (250g) green beans, trimmed
and halved crosswise*

1 garlic clove, peeled and crushed

1 tbsp chopped fresh parsley

1 tbsp shredded fresh basil

*4 tbsp French dressing
(see page 69),
made without mustard*

*1 crisp lettuce, such as Romaine
or Boston*

¼lb (100g) cherry tomatoes

*4 hard-boiled eggs, shelled,
cooled, and cut into wedges*

*14oz (400g) canned tuna in oil,
drained and broken into chunks*

*½ cup (50–75g) black olives
in oil, drained*

2oz (50g) canned anchovies in oil

*2–3 scallions, trimmed
and thinly sliced*

*saturated fat 5g • unsaturated fat 21g
sodium 989mg • calories 440*

1 Cook the potatoes in a pan of salted boiling water for 15–20 minutes, until tender.

2 Meanwhile, in another pan of salted boiling water, cook the green beans for about 3 minutes. Drain in a colander and rinse with cold water.

3 Drain the potatoes and leave them until they are cool enough to handle, then slice them. Let cool completely.

4 Add the garlic and herbs to the French dressing and whisk to mix. Check the seasoning.

5 Separate the lettuce leaves, then arrange them around the edges of four individual plates. Halve the tomatoes and place, with the eggs and potatoes, in the lettuce leaves, alternating them attractively.

6 Place the tuna in the center and surround with the olives. Drain the anchovies and arrange in a crisscross pattern on top. Scatter with the scallions and pour over the French dressing. Cover the salad loosely and chill in the refrigerator for about 1 hour before serving.

VARIATION

SALMON NIÇOISE

Replace the tuna with 4 small salmon fillets, grilled for 2 minutes on each side (see the Master Recipe on pages 92–93). Place 1 fillet in the center of each plate, omit the anchovies, and pour over the French dressing.

WARM CHICKEN LIVER SALAD

½lb (200g) package mixed
salad leaves

1lb (450g) chicken livers

3 tbsp sunflower oil

6 bacon slices, chopped

1 tbsp chopped fresh tarragon

4 tbsp French dressing
(see page 69), made
with coarse-grain mustard

croutons made from
4 slices of white or brown bread

*saturated fat 10g • unsaturated fat 37g
sodium 774mg • calories 640*

1 Tear the salad leaves into bite-sized pieces. Place them in a large salad bowl, cover with plastic wrap, and chill in the refrigerator until ready to serve.

2 If using frozen chicken livers, defrost them thoroughly, then drain in a colander for about 10 minutes.

3 Trim the livers, then place them on a double thickness of paper towels to absorb any excess liquid.

4 Heat the oil in a large nonstick sauté pan. Add the bacon and cook over low heat until it gives up its fat. Increase the heat to medium and fry until the bacon is browned and crisp. Remove with a slotted spoon and drain on paper towels.

5 Heat the oil and bacon fat remaining in the pan. Add the chicken livers and cook over high heat for no more than 3 minutes, or until the livers are well browned but still a little pink inside.

6 Remove the pan from the heat. Add the tarragon and French dressing and swirl to mix with the livers.

7 Pour the hot livers and dressing over the crisp chilled salad leaves. Add the bacon and croutons, toss together, and serve immediately.

VARIATION

WARM CHICKEN & PINE NUT SALAD

Use 2 skinless boneless chicken breasts instead of the chicken livers, and cut them into thin strips on the diagonal. Pan-fry them as for the chicken livers in the main recipe; they will take about 3 minutes to cook through. Garnish with croutons and about 2 tbsp pine nuts that have been tossed in a little olive oil over high heat for 1–2 minutes. Take care, as they burn easily.

151

FRUIT DESSERTS

Of all desserts, fruit-based ones are the most popular. Fresh and colorful, they appeal even after the richest of main courses, and if you are serving a selection of desserts a fruity one is a must.

TROPICAL FRUIT SALAD

The sugar may be left out if the fruit is sweet and ripe.

SERVES 4–6

2 thin-skinned oranges

1 grapefruit

1 small ripe melon

1 small ripe pineapple

½lb (200g) seedless black grapes, halved

¼ cup (50–75g) superfine sugar

saturated fat 0g • unsaturated fat 1g sodium 63mg • calories 247

1 Peel and segment the oranges, working over a large bowl to catch the juice. Put the segments in the bowl. Segment the grapefruit and add to the oranges.

2 Cut the melon flesh into cubes. Add to the bowl. Peel and core the pineapple. Cut the flesh into chunks and add to the bowl. Add the grapes, sprinkle with sugar if using, and stir gently to mix. Cover and chill for 2 hours before serving.

MERINGUES WITH RASPBERRY COULIS

If you sandwich the meringues together in advance, they soften. Prepare them up to 5 hours ahead.

1¼ cups (300ml) heavy cream, chilled

8 meringues (see page 36)

½ pint (200g) raspberries

4 sprigs of fresh mint, to decorate

FOR THE SAUCE

½ pint (200g) raspberries

juice of ½ lemon

confectioners' sugar, to taste

saturated fat 19g • unsaturated fat 10g sodium 55mg • calories 400

1 First make the sauce: purée the raspberries in a food processor fitted with the metal blade. Press the purée through a sieve to remove the seeds.

2 Add the lemon juice to the purée, then sweeten to taste with confectioners' sugar. Cover and chill until ready to serve.

3 Whip the cream until it is thick. Sandwich the meringues together in pairs with the cream in the middle.

4 Spoon the raspberry sauce in a pool on each of four dessert plates. Place a pair of meringues on each pool of sauce and dust with confectioners' sugar. Divide the raspberries among the plates and decorate with mint sprigs.

SEGMENTING AN ORANGE

Thin-skinned oranges have the most juice, so they are a good choice for a fruit salad. For more detailed information, see page 64.

Stand the orange upright and cut away its peel following the contours of the fruit.

Cut down between both sides of each membrane to release the orange segments.

ORANGE PASSION

This dessert can be prepared up to the end of step 2, then kept covered in the refrigerator for up to 10 hours. For a special occasion, sprinkle the oranges with brandy or Grand Marnier.

3 large thin-skinned oranges

1 cup (90g) light brown sugar

½ cup (150g) low-fat crème fraîche or light sour cream

½ cup (150g) plain yogurt

saturated fat 6g • unsaturated fat 3g
sodium 69mg • calories 254

1 Peel the oranges, then slice them crosswise into rounds. Divide the orange slices equally among four stemmed glasses or ramekins. Sprinkle with the juice from the oranges, then sprinkle each portion with 1 tsp sugar.

2 Combine the crème fraîche and yogurt in a small bowl. Spoon on top of the oranges.

3 Sprinkle the remaining sugar evenly over the cream topping. Chill in the refrigerator for 2 hours before serving.

VARIATION

MANGO PASSION

Use 1 large ripe mango instead of the oranges. Cut the mango vertically along one side of the pit, then repeat on the opposite side to make three pieces. Cut the flesh from all sides of the piece with the pit in. Remove the skin, then chop the flesh and divide it equally among the glasses. Continue as in the main recipe.

LEMON & LIME CHEESECAKE

SERVES 4–6

FOR THE CRUMB CRUST

10 graham crackers, crushed

4 tbsp butter, melted

2 tbsp light brown sugar

FOR THE FILLING

⅔ cup (150ml) heavy cream

13oz (397g) condensed milk

6oz (175g) low-fat cream cheese, at room temperature

zest and juice of 2 large lemons

zest and juice of 1½ limes

TO DECORATE

⅔ cup (150ml) heavy cream, chilled

½ lime, thinly sliced

saturated fat 25g • unsaturated fat 16g
sodium 471mg • calories 668

1 First make the crust: put the ingredients in a bowl and stir well. Turn out into an 8 in (20cm) loose-bottomed quiche tin and press firmly over the bottom and up sides using the back of a spoon. Chill for 30 minutes, until set.

2 Make the filling: put the heavy cream, condensed milk, and cream cheese in a bowl with the lemon and lime zest. Mix well. Using a balloon whisk, gradually whisk in the fruit juices and continue until mixture thickens.

3 Pour the lemon and lime filling into the crumb crust and spread it evenly. Cover and chill overnight.

4 Up to 6 hours before serving, whip the cream until it just holds its shape. Decorate the top of the cheesecake with swirls of whipped cream and slices of lime, then return to the refrigerator.

BAKED APPLES

4 large tart apples

¼ cup (50g) light brown sugar

4 tbsp butter

2 tbsp water

saturated fat 7g • unsaturated fat 4g
sodium 98mg • calories 219

1 Preheat the oven to 350°F (180°C). Core the whole apples, then make a slit in the skin around the circumference of each apple (this will prevent the apples from bursting). Place the apples in a baking dish.

2 Fill the hollow centers of the apples with the sugar, and put a knob of butter on top of each one. Pour the water into the dish. Bake for 35–40 minutes, or until the apples are soft and puffy. The sugar, butter, and water will make a syrupy sauce to spoon over the apples. Serve hot, with cream or vanilla ice cream.

VARIATION

SPICED APPLES

Fill the hollow centers of the apples with ½ cup (100g) raisins, ½ cup (75g) light brown sugar, and ¼ tsp ground cinnamon. Cook as for baked apples.

153

PLUM CRUMBLE WITH HAZELNUTS

1½ cups (750g) plums, halved and pitted

2 tbsp sugar

2 tbsp water

FOR THE CRUMBLE TOPPING

2 cups (225g) all-purpose flour

4 tbsp butter, cubed

2 tbsp granulated sugar

¾ cup (100g) toasted hazelnuts, chopped

saturated fat 15g • unsaturated fat 21g sodium 194mg • calories 680

1 Preheat the oven to 350°F (180°C). Put the plums in a baking dish measuring 8 x 10 in (20 x 25cm) and 2 in (5cm) deep. Sprinkle with the sugar and water.

2 Make the topping: put the flour in a bowl and add the butter. Rub the butter into the flour until the mixture looks like bread crumbs. Stir in the sugar and hazelnuts.

3 Scatter the crumble topping evenly over the fruit. Bake for 45 minutes, or until the topping is golden brown and the fruit juices are bubbling. Test the plums with a skewer to see if they are tender; if not, cover the crumble with foil and bake for 10–15 minutes longer. Serve warm.

VARIATION

APRICOT CRUMBLE

Omit the hazelnuts. Use apricots instead of plums and light brown sugar instead of white sugar. If you like, use half whole-wheat and half white flour.

LEMON & APPLE TART

Baking the tart on a preheated baking sheet ensures that the bottom of the pastry shell will be crisp, not soggy.

SERVES 4–6

8 in (20cm) uncooked pastry shell in its pan (see pages 66–67)

FOR THE FILLING

2 large eggs

½ cup (100g) superfine sugar

zest and juice of 1 lemon

2 tbsp butter, melted

1 large tart apple, weighing about 10oz (300g)

saturated fat 16g • unsaturated fat 15g sodium 314mg • calories 568

1 Place a baking sheet in the oven and preheat the oven to 400°F (200°C).

2 Make the filling: put the eggs and sugar in a bowl with the lemon zest and juice. Stir until evenly blended. Add the melted butter and stir to mix.

3 Peel and core the apple, then coarsely grate it directly into the bowl that contains the filling mixture. Stir well, then pour the filling into the pastry shell.

4 Set the tart in its pan on the hot baking sheet and bake for 40 minutes, or until the pastry is golden brown and the filling is slightly risen and browned. If the tart browns too much before the end of the cooking time, cover it loosely with foil and continue to cook. Serve warm.

PINEAPPLE & GINGER PAVLOVA

3 large egg whites

¾ cup (175g) superfine sugar

1 tsp vinegar

1 tsp cornstarch

1¼ cups (300ml) heavy cream, whipped

7oz (200g) canned pineapple chunks in natural juice, drained

2oz (50g) ginger in syrup, drained and finely chopped

saturated fat 19g • unsaturated fat 10g sodium 116mg • calories 513

1 Preheat the oven to 325°F (160°C). Line a baking sheet with waxed paper. Mark an 8in (20cm) circle on it.

2 Place the egg whites in a clean and dry large bowl. Using an electric mixer on full speed, beat the egg whites until they stand in stiff peaks.

3 Add the sugar 1 tsp at a time, continuing to beat on full speed until the whites are glossy. Blend the vinegar and cornstarch together and whisk into the whites with the last spoonful of sugar.

4 Spoon the meringue onto the circle on the paper and spread so the edge is slightly higher than the center. Place in the oven, turn the temperature down to 300°F (150°C), and bake for 1 hour.

5 Turn the oven off and let the pavlova cool completely in the oven. Transfer to a platter, spoon the cream in the center, and top with the pineapple and ginger.

PINEAPPLE UPSIDE-DOWN CAKE

4 tbsp butter

⅔ cup (60g) light brown sugar

5 canned pineapple rings in natural juice

15 candied cherries

FOR THE CAKE

¼lb (125g) soft margarine

½ cup (125g) superfine sugar

1½ cups (175g) self-rising flour

1 tsp baking powder

2 large eggs

*saturated fat 17g • unsaturated fat 23g
sodium 656mg • calories 765*

1 Preheat the oven to 350°F (180°C). Grease an 8in (20cm) springform pan and line the bottom with waxed paper. Melt the butter, pour it into the pan, and sprinkle with the sugar.

2 Drain the pineapple, reserving the juice. Arrange the rings in the pan, cutting them to fit as shown. Place the candied cherries in the center of the pineapple rings and between them.

3 Make the cake: place the margarine, sugar, flour, baking powder, and eggs in a large bowl. Add 2 tbsp pineapple juice. Beat with an electric mixer on slow speed for 2 minutes, or with a wooden spoon for 3–4 minutes.

4 When the mixture is soft enough to drop off the beaters or spoon, it is ready for baking. If necessary, add a few more drops of pineapple juice.

5 Spoon the cake mixture over the fruit in the pan and spread it out evenly, taking care not to dislodge the arrangement of fruit. Bake for about 45 minutes, or until the cake has risen and is springy to the touch. If the cake browns too much before the cooking time is completed, cover loosely with foil.

6 Hold a warmed plate upside down over the pan and turn the two over together so the cake inverts onto the plate.

CAKES & COOKIES

Homemade baked goods are usually reserved for special occasions, so you need to be sure of success every time. Here is a small selection of tried-and-true recipes that you can turn to again and again.

EASY FRUIT CAKE

This recipe makes a kind of fruit bread, ideal for picnics and school lunches as well as a light snack. If you wrap it tightly in waxed paper, it will keep in an airtight tin for up to 2 weeks.

CUTS INTO 12 SLICES

¾ cup (225g) soft margarine

1 cup (225g) sugar

4 large eggs

2 cups (225g) self-rising flour

¾ cup (100g) ground almonds

½ tsp almond extract

2 cups (450g) mixed dried fruit

¼ cup (25g) flaked almonds (optional)

saturated fat 6g • unsaturated fat 16g
sodium 268mg • calories 458

1 Preheat the oven to 325°F (160°C). Grease an 8in (20cm) springform cake pan. Line the bottom with waxed paper, then grease the paper.

2 Place all ingredients, except the dried fruit and almonds, in a large bowl. Beat with an electric mixer for 2–3 minutes, or with a wooden spoon for a little longer, until thoroughly mixed. Add the dried fruit and stir in with a wooden spoon.

3 Turn the mixture into the pan and smooth the top. Sprinkle with the almonds if using. Bake for 1½–2 hours. To test for doneness, insert a skewer in the center of the cake: when withdrawn, it should be clean and dry, not wet or sticky. Let the cake cool in the pan.

CHOCOLATE BROWNIES

This easy, one-stage recipe makes brownies with a cakelike texture.

MAKES 12

¾ cup (225g) soft margarine

1¾ cups (350g) light brown sugar

4 large eggs

3 tbsp cocoa powder, sifted

2 cups (250g) self-rising flour

½ tsp baking powder

½ cup (85g) walnuts (optional)

FOR THE FROSTING

3 tbsp cocoa powder, sifted

2 tbsp unsalted butter, at room temperature, cubed

4 tbsp boiling water

1¾ cups (225g) confectioners' sugar

saturated fat 8g • unsaturated fat 13g
sodium 369mg • calories 469

1 Preheat the oven to 350°F (180°C). Grease a sheet cake pan measuring 9 x 13in (23 x 33cm), line the bottom with waxed paper, then grease paper.

2 Place the margarine, sugar, eggs, cocoa powder, flour, and baking powder in a large bowl. Beat with an electric mixer on low speed for about 3 minutes, or with a wooden spoon for a little longer, until smooth. Chop the walnuts and stir in, if using.

3 Pour the mixture into the pan, spread evenly, then bake for 40–45 minutes, covering with foil for the last 10 minutes. Test with a skewer (see Easy Fruit Cake, left). Let cool in the pan until warm, then turn out onto a rack and cool completely.

4 Make the frosting: place the cocoa powder and butter in a bowl and gradually stir in the boiling water until smooth. Sift the sugar, then stir in. Let cool.

5 Spread the frosting evenly over the base with a narrow spatula. Let set, then cut into 12 x 3 in (7.5cm) squares.

BLUEBERRY MUFFINS

MAKES 12

2 large eggs

⅓ cup (85g) sugar

1 cup (225ml) milk

6 tbsp (100g) butter, melted and cooled a little

1 tsp vanilla extract

zest of 1 lemon

2¼ cups (280g) self-rising flour

1 tsp baking powder

2 cups (225g) blueberries

*saturated fat 5g • unsaturated fat 2g
sodium 211mg • calories 200*

1 Preheat the oven to 400°F (200°C). Place one paper case into each cup of a 12-cup muffin pan, to line.

2 Place the eggs, sugar, milk, melted butter, vanilla extract, and lemon zest in a large bowl and stir to combine. Sift the flour and baking powder into the bowl together. Fold the ingredients together very roughly: this should not take more than 20 strokes, and the mixture should still look lumpy and uneven. Add the blueberries and stir in.

3 Divide the mixture equally among the 12 paper cases, dropping it in from the tip of a spoon. Bake for 25–30 minutes, or until the muffins are well risen and splitting a little across the top. Transfer to a rack. Let cool slightly, but serve while still warm.

CHOCOLATE-CHIP COOKIES

MAKES 24

4 tbsp soft margarine

½ cup (100g) superfine sugar

1 large egg

1½ cups (175g) self-rising flour

½ tsp vanilla extract

½ cup (50g) semisweet chocolate chips

½ cup (50g) chopped nuts

*saturated fat 2g • unsaturated fat 3g
sodium 65mg • calories 94*

1 Preheat the oven to 350°F (180°C). Grease a baking sheet.

2 Place the margarine, sugar, egg, flour, and vanilla extract in a large bowl. Beat with an electric mixer for 2 minutes, or with a wooden spoon for a little longer, until smooth. Stir in the chocolate and nuts.

3 Divide the mixture into thirds (each third should yield 8 cookies). Use two teaspoons to scoop the mixture from the bowl and drop it onto the baking sheet. If you space the mounds about 3 in (7.5cm) apart, you will probably get 8 on the sheet at a time. With the back of a spoon, flatten each mound into a round about 2 in (5cm) in diameter.

4 Bake for 15–20 minutes, or until pale golden brown with slightly darker edges. The cookies will be only just firm to the touch. Lift carefully off the baking sheet with a narrow spatula and transfer to a rack to cool. Wipe the sheet, let it cool, and grease it again before baking the next batch.

LEMON SLICES

MAKES 16

¾ cup (225g) soft margarine

1 cup (225g) sugar

2¼ cups (275g) self-rising flour

2 tsp baking powder

4 large eggs

4 tbsp milk

zest of 2 lemons

FOR THE GLACÉ ICING

¾ cup (225g) confectioners' sugar, sifted

3 tbsp lemon juice

*saturated fat 4g • unsaturated fat 8g
sodium 242mg • calories 297*

1 Preheat the oven to 350°F (180°C). Grease a sheet cake pan measuring 9 x 13 in (30 x 23cm), line bottom with waxed paper, then grease the paper.

2 Place all the cake ingredients in a bowl. Beat with an electric mixer for 1–2 minutes, or with a wooden spoon until smooth. Turn into the pan and spread evenly.

3 Bake for 35–40 minutes, or until risen and springy to touch. Run a knife around the edge of the cake to loosen it, then turn out onto a rack and let cool.

4 Make the icing: stir the sugar and lemon juice together until smooth. Spread over the cake, let set, then cut into slices.

BREAD

Making bread and pizza is a most satisfying task. Remember

to choose a day when you know you will be at home

to keep an eye on the rising. There is very little else to do.

FARMHOUSE LOAF

4 cups (500g) all-purpose flour

2 tsp salt

1 tsp instant yeast

1¼ cups (300ml) lukewarm water

1 tbsp plus 1 tsp sunflower oil

saturated fat 3g • unsaturated fat 22g
sodium 3126mg • calories 1895

1 Measure the flour, salt, and yeast into a large bowl. Pour in the water and 1 tbsp oil and mix to a soft dough. Add 2–3 tsp more lukewarm water if necessary.

2 Put the dough onto a lightly floured surface and knead for 10 minutes.

3 Rub 1 tsp oil around a large bowl. Turn the dough in the oil, then cover bowl with plastic wrap. Let stand in a warm place for 1½ hours, or until doubled in size.

4 Grease an 8½ x 4½in (20 x 10.5cm) loaf pan. Put the dough onto the work surface and roll it into an 8 x 7in (20 x 18cm) rectangle.

5 Roll the dough from one long side. Drop it into the pan with the seam underneath. Cover with plastic wrap and let rise in a warm place for 30 minutes, or until risen 1in (2.5cm) above the pan.

6 Preheat the oven to 450°F (230°C). Bake the loaf for 10 minutes, then lower the heat to 400°F (200°C) for 30–40 minutes longer, or until golden brown. Turn the loaf out of the pan and tap it on the bottom. It should sound hollow. If not, place it upside down in the oven for a few minutes more. Cool on a rack.

VARIATIONS

OLIVE BREAD

Make the dough as in steps 1–3 of the main recipe, but replace the sunflower oil with olive oil. In step 4, work in 1 cup (100g) black and green olives, pitted and chopped, kneading them firmly into the dough until they are evenly distributed. Continue as in the main recipe.

SUN-DRIED TOMATO BREAD

Drain 1½ cups (100g) sun-dried tomatoes in olive oil, reserving the oil. Chop the sun-dried tomatoes roughly. Make the dough as in steps 1–3 of the main recipe, using the oil from the sun-dried tomatoes instead of sunflower oil. In step 4, work in the chopped sun-dried tomatoes, kneading them firmly into the dough until they are evenly distributed. Continue as in the main recipe.

ANCHOVY PIZZA

MAKES 2

2 cups (250g) all-purpose flour

1 tsp salt

½ tsp instant yeast

⅔ cup (150ml) lukewarm water

1 tbsp plus 1 tsp olive oil

FOR THE TOPPING

5oz (150g) mozzarella cheese

2oz (50g) canned anchovies in oil

6 tbsp (90ml) sun-dried tomato paste

6 pitted black olives, halved

2 tbsp olive oil

½ tsp dried oregano

saturated fat 14g • unsaturated fat 35g
sodium 2039mg • calories 1007

1 Measure the flour, salt, and yeast into a large bowl. Pour in the water and 1 tbsp oil and mix to a soft dough. Add 2–3 tsp more lukewarm water if necessary.

2 Put the dough onto a lightly floured surface and knead for 10 minutes. Rub the remaining oil around the bowl. Turn the dough in the oil, then cover the bowl with plastic wrap. Let stand in a warm place for 1½ hours, or until doubled in size.

3 Grease two baking sheets. Knead the dough for a few minutes, then divide in half. Press each piece into a 9–10in (23–25cm) round on a baking sheet, pulling the edges of the dough up so that they form a rim.

4 Drain the mozzarella and thinly slice. Drain the anchovies. Spread the tomato paste over each pizza, then top with the mozzarella, anchovies, and olives, arranging them carefully. Sprinkle with the oil and oregano. Set aside to rest.

5 Preheat the oven to 450°F (230°C). Bake for about 10 minutes, or until the pizza edges are crisp and golden, switching the baking sheets over after 5 minutes.

VARIATIONS
PEPPERONI PIZZA

Make the pizza bases as in steps 1–4 of the main recipe, then spread with the tomato paste and top with the mozzarella as in step 5. Arrange 2oz (50g) pepperoni, thinly sliced, over the mozzarella and sprinkle with ¼ cup (25g) grated Parmesan cheese and 2 tbsp sliced pickled mild chilies. Continue as in the main recipe.

TUNA PIZZA

Make the pizza bases as in steps 1–4 of the main recipe, then spread with tomato paste as in step 5. Drain and flake 7oz (200g) canned tuna in oil, then spread it over the tomato paste. Sprinkle with 1 tbsp capers, drained and chopped, 2oz (50g) mozzarella cheese, thinly sliced, ½ tsp dried oregano, and salt and pepper. Continue as in the main recipe.

COOK'S NOTES

These charts provide at-a-glance cooking times and temperatures to help you when you are cooking. On the following pages you will find information on food safety and conversion tables.

USING A THERMOMETER

When roasting meat or poultry, a meat thermometer will register the internal temperature – this is the most accurate way to gauge the degree of doneness. At the start of cooking, insert the probe of the thermometer into the thickest lean part of the meat, away from the bone. Check the temperature on the dial toward the end of cooking to see if it corresponds to the one given below.

MEAT	TEMPERATURE
LAMB	
medium rare	160–170°F (70–75°C)
well done	180°F (80°C)
BEEF	
rare	140–150°F (60–65°C)
medium	160°F (70°C)
well done	170°F (75°C)
PORK	
well done	195°F (90°C)
POULTRY	
cooked through	185°F (85°C)

DEFROSTING POULTRY

All frozen poultry must be thoroughly defrosted before cooking, or it will not cook through. Defrost birds up to 4lb (1.8kg) in a cold place overnight, or in the refrigerator for 36 hours. Birds over 4lb (1.8kg) need about 15 hours in a cold place or 48 hours in the refrigerator. Check that no ice crystals remain in the cavity before cooking.

USING A CONVECTION OVEN

Lower the temperatures in the charts by 50–70°F (10–20°C), according to your oven manufacturer's handbook.

ROASTING MEAT

TYPE	SIZE	OVEN	TIME
BEEF			
rib/sirloin	5–5.5lb (2.25–2.5kg)	400°F (200°C)	1½–1¾ hours (rare) 2–2¼ hours (medium) 2½–2¾ hours (well done)
eye round	2–4.5lb (1–2kg)	350°F (180°C)	1–1½ hours (rare) 1¾–2 hours (medium) 2¼–2½ hours (well done)
fillet (thick end)	2lb (1kg)	425°F (220°C)	30 minutes (medium rare)
	4.5lb (2kg)		40 minutes (medium rare)
LAMB			
whole leg/whole shoulder	3–5.5lb (1.5–2.5kg)	350°F (180°C)	1½–2¼ hours (medium rare) 1¾–2½ hours (well done)
half leg/half shoulder	2–3.5lb (1–1.6kg)	350°F (180°C)	1–1¾ hours (medium rare) 1½–2 hours (well done)
PORK			
loin or shoulder (boned and rolled)	2–3lb (1–1.5kg)	350°F (180°C), then 425°F (220°C)	1¾–2¼ hours (425°F/220°C for last 20 minutes)
	4.5–5.5lb (2–2.5kg)	350°F (180°C), then 425°F (220°C)	2½–3 hours (425°F/220°C for last 20 minutes)

ROASTING POULTRY

BIRD	SIZE	OVEN	TIME
CHICKEN	3–4lb (1.5–1.8kg)	400°F (200°C)	1¼–1½ hours
	5.5–6.5lb (2.5–3kg)	400°F (200°C)	2–2¼ hours
DUCK	4lb (1.8kg)	400°F (200°C), then 350°F (180°C)	45 minutes, then 1½ hours
	5.5lb (2.5kg)	400°F (200°C), then 350°F (180°C)	45 minutes, then 2 hours
TURKEY	9–11lb (4–5kg)	350°F (180°C)	3–3½ hours
	13–17.5lb (6–8kg)	350°F (180°C)	4–6 hours

GREEN VEGETABLES

■ For green vegetables with a good color, crisp bite, and maximum nutrients, cook for the minimum time in the minimum amount of water. Do not cover the pan.

■ Bring the water to a boil in a pan, add salt, then the vegetables. Start timing the moment the water returns to the boil. When the time is up, drain the vegetables in a colander. The times given here are approximate; they will vary according to the size and age of the vegetable.

BOILING GREEN VEGETABLES	
TYPE	APPROXIMATE TIME
Beans, fava, shelled	6 minutes
Beans, fine green, whole	6 minutes
Beans, thick green, sliced	5 minutes
Broccoli florets	6 minutes
Brussels sprouts, whole	6 minutes
Cabbage, leafy, shredded	3 minutes
Cauliflower, florets	6 minutes
Peas, shelled	3 minutes
Snow peas	2 minutes
Sugar snap peas	2 minutes

PASTA & RICE

■ Timings for pasta and rice depend on individual varieties and brands, so always check the box for precise instructions. Test both pasta and rice just before the end of the recommended cooking times to make sure they do not overcook. For detailed information on cooking methods, see pages 38–39.

BOILING RICE & PASTA	
TYPE	TIME
RICE	
Basmati	10–15 minutes
Brown long-grain	20–30 minutes
White long-grain	12–15 minutes
PASTA	
Dried	10–15 minutes
Dried Chinese egg noodles	6 minutes (soaking)
Fresh	2–3 minutes

ROOT VEGETABLES & SQUASH

■ Root vegetables should always be cooked in a covered pot – they are grown in the dark, underground, and so they are cooked in the dark. Acorn squash, pattypan squash, and pumpkin are cooked in the same way.

■ Put the vegetables in a saucepan, add enough cold water to cover them, then add salt. Cover the pan, bring to a boil and start timing from this moment. When the time is up, drain the vegetables in a colander.

BOILING ROOT VEGETABLES & SQUASH	
TYPE	TIME
Acorn squash, cut into chunks	15–20 minutes
Carrots, sliced/sticks	2–3 minutes
Carrots, whole young	6 minutes
Parsnips, cut into chunks	15–20 minutes
Pattypan squash, whole	6 minutes
Potatoes, cut into chunks	15–20 minutes
Potatoes, whole new	15–20 minutes
Pumpkin, cut into chunks	15–20 minutes
Rutabaga, cut into chunks	15–20 minutes
Turnips, cut into chunks	10 minutes

LEGUMES

■ All legumes, except lentils, need to be soaked overnight before cooking.

■ At the start of cooking, always boil beans and peas rapidly for 10 minutes, then drain and start again with fresh water. For detailed information on cooking methods, see page 41.

BOILING LEGUMES	
TYPE	TIME
Adzuki beans	45 minutes
Black beans	1–1½ hours
Borlotti beans	1–1½ hours
Cannellini beans	1–1½ hours
Chickpeas	2 hours
Lentils	20–30 minutes
Red kidney beans	1¼ hours
Split peas	2 hours

IT IS IMPORTANT to handle and store perishable foods with care, so they can be enjoyed at their best, and to help prevent food poisoning. Buy from a reputable retailer, first checking the expiration date. Take fresh food home and put it in the refrigerator or freezer as soon as possible. Keep work surfaces, utensils, and hands clean. Separate cutting boards should be kept for raw and cooked foods, but if this is not possible, wash boards thoroughly between each use. These guidelines are a matter of common sense and apply to all fresh food, but some foods need special care – these are dealt with below.

CHEESE
■ Cheeses made from unpasteurized milk, especially soft cheeses, soft mature cheeses (pasteurized and unpasteurized), and blue-veined cheeses, should not be eaten by pregnant women, babies, young children, the sick, and the elderly. These people are at greater risk from the listeria bacteria, which may be present in these cheeses.

EGGS
■ Always buy fresh eggs from a reputable store, first checking that the shells are clean and uncracked. Look for eggs that have the expiration date stamped on the carton so that you know they are fresh and how long it is safe to store them.
■ Store eggs, pointed ends down, in the refrigerator, away from strong-smelling foods.
■ Always wash hands thoroughly before and after handling raw eggs.
■ If an egg is contaminated with the salmonella bacteria, the risk of contracting salmonella poisoning is higher if the egg is raw, has a runny yolk, or is softly set, so avoid serving these to pregnant women, babies and young children, and the sick and elderly. For the salmonella bacteria to be destroyed, the egg must be cooked to 160°F (71°C), the temperature at which an egg yolk sets.

DRIED BEANS & PEAS
■ These legumes, especially red kidney beans, may contain harmful toxins that can cause food poisoning.
■ Always boil dried beans and peas rapidly for a full 10 minutes at the start of the cooking time, then drain and start again with fresh water.

MEAT
■ Always buy fresh meat from a reputable source and refrigerate it as soon as possible after purchase, first removing any plastic wrappings, drip trays, etc. Put fresh meat on a plate or in a bowl, cover it, and place it at the bottom of the refrigerator.
■ Store raw and cooked meats separately and never handle them together. Wash surfaces, utensils, and hands before, between, and after dealing with raw and cooked meats.
■ Frozen meat should be defrosted thoroughly before cooking. Throw the thawed liquid away and do not refreeze raw meat.
■ Reheat previously cooked meat dishes only once. Make sure they are thoroughly reheated until boiling or piping hot (above 170°F/75°C).

MUSSELS & CLAMS
■ Buy live mussels and clams from a reputable source, and cook them on the day of purchase.
■ Before cooking, discard any with broken shells or open shells that do not close when sharply tapped. These are not safe to eat. After cooking, discard any that are not open. These may not be safe either.

POTATOES
■ If potatoes have been exposed to light during storage, they may develop green patches, so always store them in the dark as soon as possible after purchase.
■ Small green patches on the skin of potatoes can be cut out with a peeler or knife, but if the greening covers a large area, it is advisable to throw the potato away. Greening can cause gastrointestinal distress.

POULTRY
■ Refrigerate whole birds and pieces as quickly as possible after purchase. Remove any wrappings, and any giblets from the cavity of whole birds, then put the poultry on a plate, cover loosely, and store in the bottom of the refrigerator away from any cooked poultry or meat. Refrigerate any giblets separately in a covered bowl.
■ Poultry is particularly susceptible to contamination by salmonella. Wash work surfaces, utensils, and hands thoroughly before and after handling, and do not let the raw bird or any equipment come into contact with cooked poultry or meat.
■ Defrost all birds thoroughly before cooking (for times, see page 160). Do not refreeze.
■ Do not stuff a bird until just before cooking: make sure the stuffing is cold, stuff only the neck end, not the cavity, and keep the stuffing loose.
■ Cook the bird thoroughly to kill any bacteria. At the end of cooking, insert a skewer in the thigh: if properly cooked, the juices should be clear, not pink. Test a large bird with a meat thermometer – the internal temperature should be 185°F (85°C).

RICE (COOKED)
■ Always store any leftover cooked rice in a covered container in the refrigerator; never leave it in an uncovered pot or bowl at room temperature. Bacteria, which can cause gastrointestinal problems, can grow in cooked rice if it is not stored at a temperature below 39°F (4°C) (the temperature of your refrigerator should be between 32–39°F/0–4°C). When reheating cooked rice, make sure it is very hot.

NUTRITIONAL INFORMATION

THE RECIPES in the Master Recipes and Recipe Repertoire sections give values for fat, sodium, and calories. All figures are approximate and are based on figures from food composition tables with additional data for manufactured products. They are intended as a guide only and not as an absolute amount. All recipes have been analyzed with no added salt, unless a specific amount is given in the recipe. The use of salt to taste will result in widely varying sodium levels. Garnishes and ingredients that are described as "to serve" or "optional" are not included in the nutritional analysis.

CONVERSION CHARTS

OVEN TEMPERATURES

■ Always preheat the oven: if the oven is not preheated before the food goes in, results may not be successful. Recipes in this book have been tested in a preheated oven.

■ The temperatures given in this book are Fahrenheit and Celsius. The chart at right gives the equivalents for easy reference. No two ovens are alike, so you may need to adjust temperatures and/or cooking times to suit your oven. For convection ovens, lower the temperatures in the chart by 50–68°F (10–20°C), according to the manufacturer's handbook.

FAHRENHEIT	CELSIUS	OVEN HEAT
225°	110°	very cool
250°	120°	very cool
275°	140°	cool
300°	150°	cool
325°	160°	moderate
350°	180°	moderate
375°	190°	moderately hot
400°	200°	moderately hot
425°	220°	hot
450°	230°	very hot

WEIGHTS & MEASURES

■ All the weights, volumes, and measurements in this book are in imperial and metric. The charts at right give the equivalents for easy reference. The two are not interchangeable, so use imperial only or metric only, and never mix them.

■ Tablespoon and teaspoon measures used in this book are expressed as tbsp and tsp, and fractions of these. Recipes have been tested using a set of accurate measuring spoons (see page 26), and spoons are always level unless otherwise stated.

METRIC	SPOON
15ml	1 tbsp
5ml	1 tsp
2.5ml	½ tsp
1.25ml	¼ tsp

WEIGHT		VOLUME		MEASUREMENTS	
IMPERIAL	METRIC	IMPERIAL	METRIC	IMPERIAL	METRIC
½oz	15g	½ cup	125ml	¼in	5mm
1oz	25g	⅔ cup	150ml	½in	1cm
2oz	50g	¾ cup	175ml	1in	2.5cm
3oz	75g	1 cup	250ml	2in	5cm
4oz	100g	1⅛ cups	275ml	3in	7cm
6oz	175g	1¼ cups	300ml	4in	10cm
7oz	200g	1½ cups	350ml	5in	12cm
8oz	250g	1¾ cups	400ml	6in	15cm
9oz	275g	1⅞ cups	450ml	7in	18cm
10oz	300g	2 cups	500ml	8in	20cm
12oz	350g	2½ cups	600ml	9in	23cm
1lb	500g	3 cups	750ml	10in	25cm
1½lb	750g	3¾ cups	900ml	11in	28cm
2lb	1kg	4 cups	1 liter	12in	30cm

Page numbers in bold indicate Techniques or Master Recipes; those in italics indicate dishes from the Recipe Repertoire and variations.
An asterisk (*) indicates savory recipes suitable for vegetarians (replacing chicken stock with vegetable stock where necessary).

U V

W

X Y Z

ACKNOWLEDGMENTS

FOOD PREPARATION AND RECIPE TESTING
Caroline Liddell

DK would like to thank Fay Franklin for editorial management, Virginia Walter for design management, Mari Roberts for editorial assistance, Robert Ford and Laura Jackson for design assistance, Susan Bosanko for the index, Jasmine Challis for the nutritional information, and the British Chicken Information Service and the Meat and Livestock Commission for their helpful advice and information.
Additional photography by David Murray and Jules Selmes, Jerry Young, Amanda Heywood, Clive Streeter, Philip Dowell, Stephen Oliver, and Steve Gorton.

Special thanks also go to the following companies for their generous gifts: Schwartz Herbs and Spices for the supply of the herbs and spices on pages 14–16; Lakeland Plastics Ltd. of Windermere, Cumbria, for the supply of a wide range of kitchen equipment; ICTC of Norwich for pots, pans, and utensils; Jim Wilkinson Promotions Ltd. for the Good Grips potato masher.
Thanks also to the following for their kind loans: Magimix UK Ltd. for the blender and food processor; Kenwood Appliances plc for the food mixer; Braun (UK) Ltd. for the handheld blender; David Mellor for various items; and Divertimenti for various items.